SCHOOL LAW
YEARBOOK

Reference Guide to
Education Law

Aspen's Administration Development Group

From the editors of *Education Daily*

AN ASPEN PUBLICATION®
Aspen Publishers, Inc.
Gaithersburg, Maryland
2000

S0-ARN-089

Copyright © 2000 by Aspen Publishers, Inc.
A Wolters Kluwer Company
www.aspenpublishers.com
All rights reserved.

Jane Garwood, Publisher
Jo Gulledge, Executive Director
             Acquisitions, Education
Dave Harrison, Executive Editor, Education
Esmeralda Barnes, Editor, *School Law News*
Rosette Graham, Senior Production Manager
Jennifer Barnes Eliot, Marketing Manager

Orders: 800-638-8437
Customer Service: 800-234-1660
ISBN: 0-8342-1867-4

About Aspen Publishers • For more than 40 years, Aspen has been a leading
professional publisher in a variety of disciplines. Aspen's vast information resources are available in both print and electronic formats. We are committed
to providing the highest quality information available in the most appropriate
format for our customers. Visit Aspen's Internet site for more information resources,directories, articles, and a searchable version of Aspen's full catalog, including the most recent publications: **www.aspenpublishers.com**
     Aspen Publishers, Inc. • The hallmark of quality in publishing
                Member of the worldwide Wolters Kluwer group.

Printed in the United States of America

1 2 3 4 5

Table of Contents

Introduction

In the 1990s, school law issues seemed to materialize and evaporate with alarming quickness.

When the '90s kicked in, it seemed every school district was concerned about whether—and how—to mainstream special education students into regular classes. By the middle of the decade, though, sexual harassment and gender bias cases were perplexing schools and school attorneys.

Now, a new decade has brought a new set of issues. Only time will tell how long it will take courts to settle these recent legal dilemmas, what their ultimate impact will be on students and schools, and what new problems will inevitably follow.

The U.S. Supreme Court's pending decision on whether prayers before football games at public schools violate the First Amendment is the most highly awaited ruling of the 1999-2000 session, especially since it will break the high court's decade-long silence on the issue.

But legal observers are also closely watching pending cases challenging the use of race in student school assignments and the general issue of federal-versus-state supremacy on a variety of issues affecting schools.

* * *

The spectrum of cases on religion in the realm of public schools reflects the many legal and philosophical differences at the root of conflicts over what constitutes a violation of the First Amendment's Establishment Clause, which bans government endorsement of religion.

The last time the high court spoke on a major school religion case was in its 1992 *Lee v. Weisman* opinion (112 S. Ct. 2649), in which it held that invocations and benedictions at graduation ceremonies are unconstitutional.

Now, it is set to decide whether prayers before football games are legal. The case is *Santa Fe Independent School District v. Doe*, in which the Texas school district is seeking to overturn a 5th Circuit Court of Appeals decision that barred it from allowing prayer before the games.

The high court has yet to rule on whether student-led prayers are legal, and courts around the country have been issuing conflicting rulings on the matter.

In an opposite ruling from the Texas case, an 11th Circuit opinion held that schools are free to allow student-led prayers with religious content at football games, graduations or other occasions that don't occur during classtime.

Whether the Supreme Court will set in stone legal principles of the past 25 years—or alter them dramatically—is the question on the minds of legal observers, who all agree a high court resolution on this thorny issue is long overdue.

An element of resolution in this area of law is expected with the high court's pending decision regarding what level of public aid to religious schools is acceptable. *Mitchell v. Helms* puts to the test a federal program in Louisiana that provides computers, televisions, library materials and other supplies to parochial schools.

The case went before the high court last December, and a ruling is expected before summer.

Courts around the country have grappled with how to apply the Supreme Court's precedents banning the use of publicly funded school vouchers, tax credits and other programs that allow parents to send their children to religious schools on taxpayer dollars.

But the high court has not yet acted to settle the fractious debate over government support of private, religious schools.

In October 1999, without comment, the justices let stand two cases from Maine that allows the state to use public funds to pay tuition for children at secular schools while denying the same support to those attending religious schools. A federal court in Vermont issued a similar ruling.

The conflict among federal circuits continues, with federal rulings in Wisconsin and Arizona conflicting with those in Maine and Vermont. The high court has rejected appeals from those states.

While the *Mitchell* case is not a voucher case—it deals instead with direct public aid to parochial schools—experts expect the upcoming ruling to shed some legal light on the court's take on the general issue of public support of private schools.

* * *

Another major issue before the court is racially based school assignments. The court has not acted yet on two recently filed appeals over the use of race in admissions and in determining school transfers in Virginia and Maryland, respectively.

The first case, *Tuttle v. Arlington County School Board* (98-604), is an appeal from the 4th Circuit Court of Appeals declaring illegal the practice of using race in admissions via a lottery at a popular Arlington, Va., school.

Although many legal experts are not hopeful that the largely conservative high court will break the chain of anti-affirmative action rulings from federal courts, an element of the lower court decision in *Tuttle* gives school officials some hope for the future of their embattled diversity policy.

The appeals court's three-judge panel advised the school to use another policy more tailored than the lottery to increasing diversity without favoring minority students. The lottery was one of several options for boosting diversity crafted by a county committee.

The other options included assigning a portion of students living in some minority neighborhoods to the school, opening the lottery to all incoming kindergartners in the county, and giving students from each neighborhood a set number of seats.

The second case seeking a high court nod is *Eisenberg v. Montgomery County Public Schools*. Last October, the 4th Circuit Court of Appeals ruled illegal a Maryland school district's policy of not allowing children to transfer to a new school if the previous school would be worse off with respect to racial diversity.

These cases mark a modern-day wave of legal actions taken by white parents who argue their children are being disadvantaged by efforts to maintain diversity at public schools.

One recent move by a Boston school district exemplifies school districts' unease with the use of race in admissions.

Last July, Boston ended initiatives aimed at maintaining racial balance mandated by court order two decades ago. City school officials feared they would not successfully defend their efforts in light of lower court decisions declaring their diversity programs illegal.

Still, school officials in Maryland and Virginia are hoping the Supreme Court justices will overturn decisions barring their respective programs. High court appeals in those cases were filed last December.

That's a chance that Boston officials—with full approval by the National Association for the Advancement of Colored People—were unwilling to take, fearing the court's conservative, anti-affirmative action bent would set a national, legal precedent against the programs they credit with guarding the modest gains of past desegregation efforts.

But lawyers close to the Virginia and Maryland cases say their cases may fare better because—rather than arguing that the race-based admissions program is necessary to remedy past effects of segregation, as Boston officials contend—they tout such admissions practices as serving a "compelling educational interest."

That "interest" means considering race as a factor in determining admissions and maintaining diversity in school enrollments by monitoring racial balance are important education tools in offering *all* students a balanced education, the attorneys say.

That legal argument generally was affirmed in the high court's *Regents of the University of California v. Bakke* (438 U.S. 265). It held that race could be used as one factor in admissions—but it could not be the only factor—and there must be a compelling reason to use it.

The argument that such programs are necessary to remedy past discrimination, as was held in the Boston case, has failed in the 5th Circuit, where an appeals court ruled that race could be considered in efforts to remove bias at schools, but not society at large. The Supreme Court let stand *Texas v. Hopwood* (95-1773) in the 5th Circuit states of Louisiana, Texas and Mississippi.

Court cases since *Hopwood* have followed the Texas case's narrow interpretation of *Bakke,* setting a high standard for what is a valid use of race in various school policies and declaring many of those policies illegal.

The result is what some call erosion of desegregation gains spurred by white parents or students fighting to regain educational opportunities they see as lost to affirmative action.

Though the parents and students have been winning the battles in federal courts across the country, the Supreme Court may have to decide who wins the war.

* * *

School attorneys say they also are watching the ongoing battle between states' rights and federal authority.

While these cases generally encompass issues well-beyond schools, the high court's pro-states rulings, affirming states' authority while limiting federal intrusion, affect a number of school-related issues.

For example, the Supreme Court ruled in January that Congress overstepped its authority when it passed the 1967 Age Discrimination in Employment Act, allowing federal age-discrimination suits against states and their agencies.

Legal experts say a key issue will be how the court continues to curb federal authority in state affairs. As one legal expert said, "It will effect schools from the standpoint of 'Who is your boss: Congress or the state?'"

Beyond these issues, experts predict the timely, ever-evolving school safety cases, challenging everything from drug testing to search-and-seizure policies, will continue to fill federal dockets—along with cases stemming from the emotional, mammoth realm of special education—vying for a coveted review from the nation's highest court.

CHAPTER 1

Affirmative Action

Over the past 40 years, affirmative action has forced a revolution in education reform that has morphed a historic race debate.

Equal-educational opportunities for minority students once dominated
the collective consciousness of school policymakers, regardless of their
views on the issue. And that was because black parents and their supporters filed multiple lawsuits, held protests and shouted from every
high place that black children would not be denied educational opportunities.

Those efforts paid off, as court-mandated desegregation orders forced
states to address historical inequities between black and white students
in classroom instruction, facilities and other educational resources.

Decades later—despite the contention of many minorities that desegregation efforts are incomplete, and that minority achievement is still re-
covering from the effects of segregation—white parents and students are
doing the shouting, and filing the lawsuits.

In multiple lawsuits of late, they have sued and defeated school districts
arguing that affirmative action—the use of race in school admissions or
financial aid—is robbing *their* children of equal-educational opportunity, violating the Equal Protection Clause of the U.S. Constitution.

The new affirmative action debate may be characterized in these words:
equal-educational opportunity at what cost?

And that is a question officials from many school districts are asking
themselves, when weighing their stated need to use race-based admis-

sions policies for diversity in enrollments against a bleak legal track record of losing in the courts.

Many find it more advantageous, both financially and educationally, simply to change their policies to create more egalitarian ways of filling classrooms in their selective and prestigious programs and schools.

The modern-day affirmative action debate has spawned a number of lawsuits, including one by a school district stepping back from not only affirmative action in enrollments but also forced busing.

When a federal appeals court in December 1998 ruled that Boston's admissions policy at the prestigious Boston Latin School was illegal, local officials considered taking their case to the U.S. Supreme Court.

But on second thought, given the cost of litigation, and—as one Boston official put it—"the conservative tilt of the U.S. Supreme Court," officials relented. Instead, they opted to move to a race-neutral admissions policy for Boston Latin and the city's two other exam schools.

Ultimately, the white student who challenged Boston's policy after having been denied entrance to the prestigious Boston Latin school was one of a handful to successfully challenge these race policies.

* * *

Diversity among teaching staffs is another element of this contentious debate, with school districts grappling with how to diversify their ranks—purportedly to provide minority students with role models of their own race—without trumping anti-discrimination-in-employment laws.

The U.S. Supreme Court set the legal precedent on this issue in a 1986 case that held it illegal to maintain a set number of minority teachers in the interest of providing role models to minority teachers.

The evolution of legal cases in the last half century—from the black parents of the landmark *Brown* case to the white parents of the modern reverse-discrimination case *Capacchione*—has spawned new (but difficult and elusive) lessons for school administrators.

Court rulings reflect that, at the very least, race policies should be narrowly tailored to remedy the present effects of past discrimination and have no discriminatory purpose. For example, courts have found the following programs illegal:

- voluntary transfer programs limiting the number of students based on race;

- magnet or higher education admission programs and scholarships that separate students by race and apply separate admissions standards; and

- policies forbidding student busing with exceptions for almost every reason except race.

But courts have ruled legal the following:

- admissions policies that require an enrollment composition of half blacks and half whites;

- recruitment programs that have no effect on admissions criteria; and

- teacher certification programs that do not set up separate criteria for teachers based on race.

Perhaps a school attorney speaking at the 1999 Education Law Association conference best summarized the current state of affirmative action in education:

"Even though jurisprudence has evolved considerably in this area, unanswered questions remain about the use of race-based criteria to determine student admission and assignment," said Denise Nance Pierce of the Texas law firm of Bickerstaff, Heath, Smiley, Pollan, Kever & McDaniel.

"Public school officials across the country right now lack clear and definitive guidance for managing, continuing or dismantling race-based student assignment and admissions plans.

"It may nearly require another half century for the federal courts to sort out the remaining questions and to complete the full circle of analysis

on the application of the Equal Protection Clause to race-based deci-
sion-making in public school admissions and assignments," Pierce said.

ENROLLMENT

NAACP, San Francisco Schools Settle Race Case

The NAACP and San Francisco schools last year settled a federal case
that helped determine the constitutionality of race-based admissions at
elite city schools.

Although some details of the January 1999 settlement were sealed by
the court, it repeals court-ordered limits on racial and ethnic groups at
each school in the 63,000-pupil school system.

A 1983 court order resolved a 1978 discrimination suit from the NAACP
against the San Francisco school system by imposing a 45 percent ceil-
ing on any racial or ethnic group at a public school. The limit at alternative or magnet schools, which offer special programs and require admissions exams, is 40 percent.

But the three Chinese-American families who sued the district over the
policy in 1994 said it kept their children out of their preferred schools,
including the prestigious Lowell High School, despite their strong academic standings.

Separate Standards

The schools' admissions policy at the time required Chinese-Americans,
the largest minority group in Lowell's enrollment, to score higher than
other ethnic groups.

Under the Feb. 16 settlement, the district would be prohibited from
assigning students based on race or ethnicity but could consider socio-economic status, according to state education officials familiar
with the draft.

The settlement in *Ho v. San Francisco Unified School District* (94-2418) was
reached the same day the trial was set to begin in the U.S. District Court

for the Northern District of California. The case comes as circuits across the country are ruling against similar race-based admissions practices. The U.S. First Circuit Court of Appeals in November upheld a lower court decision that struck down a race-based admissions policy at a prestigious public high school in Boston.

Citing the climate in the courts against such practices, Boston school officials opted not to appeal the decision to the Supreme Court.

Federal Court Rejects K-12 Race-Based Admissions

A federal appeals court barred the use of racial preferences at Boston's most prestigious high school, and the city last year agreed not to appeal the ruling.

Henry Robert Wessman challenged Boston Latin School's admissions policy when his daughter Sarah, 15, who is white, was refused admission to the 2,300-student school. He charged that the school had illegally denied her admission in favor of less qualified minorities.

The magnet school, which enrolls students throughout the district, selects half of them based on academic achievement and the other half on a weighted race formula that requires the percentage of minority students admitted to equal the percentage of minority applicants whose records place them at the top of their class.

Following the court's December 1998 ruling, the Boston School Committee voted last February not to appeal the decision.

"Given the conservative tilt of the U.S. Supreme Court, we decided, after talking to many experts around the country, that the likelihood of the practice being overturned(and dismantling other programs around the country—was great," said Elizabeth Reilinger, chairwoman of the Boston School Committee. "Moving forward would have been detrimental to similar programs," she said in explaining the board's unanimous vote that reversed the committee's earlier plan to appeal to the Supreme Court.

A school task force comprising school staff and independent experts will review new race-neutral admissions policies for the exclusive

Boston Latin School and the city's two other exam schools. Officials expect school staff to report to the committee by late summer.

In the meantime, students seeking admissions to one of the three schools this fall were evaluated based on test scores and grade-point average, school officials said. But students seeking admission for the 2000-01 school year will be admitted using a new policy that "passes constitutional muster," said school spokeswoman Tracey Lynch.

Plan Doesn't Pass Muster

But the 2-to-1 decision by the U.S. First Circuit Court of Appeals, in *Wessman v. Gittans, et al.* (98-1657), overturned a May 1998 federal district court decision and ordered Boston Latin to admit Sarah.

Wessman's attorney, Michael McLaughlin, said the decision represented a "complete rejection of the policy of the Boston School Committee and a complete vindication for us."

"The court effectively made a strong statement that forcing a school's enrollment to reflect the racial balance of the school system is unconstitutional, even if it is called diversity," he added.

Legal experts say the case propels the volatile affirmative action debate from colleges and universities at the K-12 level.

A series of federal rulings over the past decade have struck down affirmative action policies at colleges and universities nationwide. The most recent ruling came two years ago when the U.S. Fifth Circuit Court of Appeals banned the use of race in university admissions at the University of Texas law school. The U.S. Supreme Court refused to hear the case, letting stand the lower court decision.

But race-based admissions practices at prestigious public schools pose a different constitutional dilemma, experts say, because like Boston, many districts have spent decades under court order to integrate their schools. Magnet schools such as Boston Latin often are set up to give integration a boost.

The Boston Latin ruling affects schools in Maine, Massachusetts, New Hampshire, Rhode Island and Puerto Rico, but it will attract the attention of officials in other districts, such as Arlington, Va., where race-based admissions practices have been challenged.

In Arlington, a lottery-based admissions system that favors black, Hispanic and low-income students over white students was twice struck down as unconstitutional in rulings from the U.S. District Court for the Eastern District of Virginia. Arlington school officials are appealing that decision, and the U.S. Justice Department filed a brief backing the school district.

San Diego Schools Drop Race in Admissions

The San Diego Board of Education voted this January to exclude race as a factor in admitting students to magnet schools.

The 20-year-old policy had been aimed at maintaining diversity in school enrollments while offering various educational programs.

But recent court decisions have held such programs unconstitutional. So, like many officials from other cities, the board opted to revise the policy on Jan. 25, 2000.

"We may not escape litigation, but what we have done, we have done in a manner of consensus," Superintendent Alan Bersin said.

The new policy divides the city into four clusters. Students now get priority in admissions based on residence and socioeconomics.

"The challenge has been in creating a program that eliminates race as a criteria but would not segregate our schools," said the district's integration program manger, Pat Trandal.

"I think you will find a close correlation across the country between race, socioeconomics and geography," she said. Students will get higher priority in enrollment if they apply to a magnet school in a cluster with different demographics than the one in which they live.

BUSING

Court Battles Abound As Schools Pursue Diversity

As federal courts move to release cities from federal desegregation mandates, districts seeking to maintain racial balance in schools are finding themselves back in court.

But this time, the parents of white students are filing lawsuits, arguing that school systems' dogged pursuit of racial balance, diversity and equal educational opportunity for all students has denied their children the same equality districts claim to be preserving for all children.

Some districts have chosen to fight those lawsuits, saying that the steps taken to preserve racial balance in schools is not only necessary but also mandatory to sustain the positive gains brought by previous court-ordered integration efforts.

Other school districts—most recently Boston—are opting not to fight those lawsuits, seeing them as costly, time-consuming and ultimately distracting from the behemoth, modern-day task of boosting student achievement despite formidable socio-economic odds.

Boston school officials last July voted 5-2 to end a quarter century of busing, a move that has sparked much debate in the education community about integration and its legacy in education reform.

Harvard education professor and civil rights expert Gary Orfield said that Boston and other cities in recent years have made a mistake seeking "unitary status," a term that refers to a court's declaration that a previously segregated or dual school system has essentially reached its goal of integration.

"Before obtaining unitary status, a school district has the legal right to do what it needs to reduce segregation," said Orfield, who last month published a study that said racial segregation is making a comeback.

After unitary status, local politics—rather than the courts—rules. "Too many school districts are seeking unitary status without knowing what it is or the legal challenges it often brings," he said.

Washington, D.C., civil rights attorney William L. Taylor pointed to a number of recent lawsuits in various stages of litigation that sprang from school districts' efforts to maintain integration. They include:

- *Wessman v. Gittens* (98-1657): White parents sued Boston school officials over race-based admissions policy at the Boston Latin School; the 1st Circuit Court of Appeals ruled the practice unconstitutional. The school board opted not to appeal.

- *Rosenfeld v. Montgomery County Public Schools* (98-1793): White parents sued Montgomery County Public Schools for using racial preferences in deciding admission at a magnet school. The case is awaiting appeal at the 4th Circuit Court of Appeals. A federal district court rejected the parents' claim under Title VI of the Civil Rights Act, but allowed the parents to sue for due process violations.

- *Brewer v. West Irondequoit Central School District* (98-6393): Parents of a white elementary student sued the district over a school transfer program that allows only minority students in a mostly black school district to transfer to mostly white suburban schools. The U.S. District Court for the Western District of New York held that the policy violated the white student's constitutional equal protection rights. The case is on appeal.

- *Eisenberg v. Montgomery County Public Schools* (98-2797): A white parent sued the school district over a policy that bars children from transferring from a school if the departure disrupts the school's racial balance. The U.S. District Court for the District of Maryland, Southern Division, ruled in favor of the school district. The parent appealed, and the case is pending at the 4th Circuit Court of Appeals.

Case Watch

These and other cases are being watched closely because the U.S. Supreme Court has not ruled on whether elementary and secondary schools are permitted to impose admissions restrictions to maintain or achieve racial balance. But, Taylor said, "the court said clearly in a 1971 high court decision that school districts have the authority to adopt a program to achieve racially balanced schools for the purpose of living in a racially balanced society."

The landmark case was *Swann v. Charlotte-Mecklenburg Board of Education* (402 U.S. 1), and it cleared the way for nationwide busing.

More than 30 years later, the city school district found itself in federal court again because white parents sued over the school district's use of racial criteria in admitting students to a magnet school.

A Continuing Saga

Though there are hundreds of districts in various stages in desegregation lawsuits, in recent years, a number of cities have won release from federal court-ordered busing programs, including Indianapolis; Kansas City, Mo.; Denver; Oklahoma City; Norfolk, Va.; Wilmington, Del.; Nashville; Cleveland; and Boston.

"But just as schools are getting out from under desegregation orders, the issue is surfacing in the context of charter schools," said Clint Bolick, litigation director of the Institute for Justice in Washington, D.C.

Bolick's group is preparing to join a legal fight in East Baton Rouge, La., where a group called Children's Charter garnered local approval to set up a charter school for academically struggling minority students.

Bolick said the Justice Department is fighting the establishment of the charter school, citing a long-standing desegregation order that requires all public schools to maintain racial balance. Justice's apparent concern is that the charter school will enroll the few white students attending predominantly black schools.

In a filing in the case last July, the Justice Department asked a federal court to require that the school district seek court approval before acting or funding any charter schools, and base the approval of any charter school on the condition that desegregation efforts will not be negatively affected.

"Why should children be penalized under the same desegregation orders meant to help them achieve academically?" Bolick asked.

Justice spokeswoman Christine DiBartolo, echoing the filing, said Justice does not directly oppose the charter school, but it opposes any action that would "impede desegregation efforts" or violate the district's legal obligation to seek court approval before approving any new schools."

Boston Vote Reflects Complexities of Reform

More than 30 years ago, the one-word thrust of education reform proved simple in theory and complicated in practice: integration.

Today, the complexity remains, but the nature of reform is facing a revolutionary redefinition of terms, leaving unanswered questions that continue to bedevil school districts, courts and citizens: What is equal educational opportunity? When has it been established? And how "equal" is it, if it helps one racial group to the apparent detriment of another?

Boston schools officials tackled that conundrum last July, when the Boston School Committee voted to end its landmark busing initiative mandated by a federal court 27 years ago to remedy educational disparities among blacks and whites caused by segregation.

But the debate is far from over—for Boston or the nation. As federal courts release from their oversight school districts that previously faced mandates to integrate black students and improve their education, those same districts are facing lawsuits, stemming from what the districts view as their best efforts to maintain racial balance in their schools.

The lawsuits typically come from white parents who feel their children were wrongly denied a slot at the school of their choice, were wrongly assigned to a particular school, or were not allowed to transfer from one school to another in the name of racial balance. But for some districts, such as Boston, the lawsuits are too costly and time-consuming to merit the fight, particularly when court rulings on the issue often are unpredictable and mixed.

Boston school system officials said the 5-2 vote by the mayor-appointed school committee members was prompted by a lawsuit filed a month earlier by white parents who claimed the city's policy discriminated against their children.

The vote means that in the fall of 2000, the city will abandon its "controlled choice" program, in which parents get some say on where their children attend school but race is also a factor in assignments.

Race will not be a factor in a child's school assignment. A student's residence in relation to the location of a school, sibling placements and the results of a yearly school choice lottery will determine that.

Both Boston Mayor Thomas Menino and city School Superintendent Thomas Payzant said they feared that the old system—which used race in assigning students to schools as a means of maintaining racial balance in enrollments—would not have survived a legal challenge.

They pointed to a federal court ruling last December in favor of a white parent who claimed the city's admissions quota at its prestigious Boston Latin School was unconstitutional.

City school officials briefly considered appealing the ruling to the U.S. Supreme Court, but later opted to drop race as an admissions factor rather than allow the likely defeat of its program—"given the conservative tilt of the U.S. Supreme Court"—to set a national standard.

But it's the school committee's reasoning for dropping its voluntary busing plan that has some lawyers and experts reeling.

A 'Craven' Act

Washington, D.C., civil rights attorney William Taylor had this to say: "The first question I have for Payzant is what makes him so sure that he is avoiding a legal battle. How does he know he won't be sued by those who oppose the dismantling of the busing plan and think it's illegal?"

Taylor said his comments are "more than rhetorical" because lawsuits could come from either side of the issue. "As far as I know, Boston is the first school district to abandon desegregation efforts because it feared lawsuits," he said. "I think it's craven on the part of a school district to give up on desegregation plans because it's afraid it's going to be sued."

A New Era

But Mayor Menino said racial issues have distracted from improving teaching and student achievement, two issues that should be the city schools' main goals. And Superintendent Payzant said, "It's time to move on. It's not the '70s. It's not the '80s. It's the end of the '90s."

They both also pointed out that Boston has changed greatly since the 1974 federal order that sparked violent protests from white parents because it forced their children to ride buses into black neighborhoods and vice versa.

More than 25 years ago, minority students made up 48 percent of the public school enrollment in Boston, and schools were either all-white or all-black.

Today, due to the "white flight" out of the city during the last three decades and the growing immigrant population, city schools are now 85 percent minority, officials said. Forty-nine percent of the enrollment is black; 26 percent, Hispanic; and 9 percent, Asian.

The demographic result of the committee's action is that just eight of the city's 129 schools would see an increase of no more than 10 white students, and one school would see an increase of no more than 15 whites, Payzant said.

Payzant said he plans to build six new schools in neighborhoods that do not have enough schools for children. His goal is that, in six years, every student will be within walking distance of a school.

City officials also said the gains of integration in part will be guarded by a 1974 state law, the Racial Imbalance Law, which requires that schools with at least 50 percent minority students craft a plan to create racial balance.

No Comfort for the Leery

"It's a terrible decision … that placed Boston out of the position of being a role model for achieving fairness for all racial groups," said Charles Willie, a Harvard education professor who designed the controlled choice plan for Boston and other Massachusetts cities.

His fear is the city will become segregated again, in spite of officials' contentions that the city's diversity will guard against that. "That's a lie," he said. "They know it, and all the people who have any understanding of the population distribution know it. The neighborhoods in Boston are not integrated."

State Sen. Dianne Wilkerson represents some of the city's majority-black areas. While there is much work to do to ensure equitable educational quality among Boston's schools, she said, the fact that blacks and white joined to support the new proposal shows marked progress, compared with the city's volatile days 25 years ago.

Three of the five school committee members who voted for the end of busing, are black.

The Boston School Committee's vote did not placate the white parents who want Boston to abandon race as a factor in student assignments immediately. In fact, Chester Darling, attorney for the Boston parents' group that filed the lawsuit prompting the vote, said they plan to press for an immediate end to busing. But a federal district judge did not act on the parents' request to block the program for the 1999-2000 school year.

Clint Bolick of the Institute for Justice said the critics of Boston's action and others like it "have it exactly backwards."

"The result of busing in city after city has been to expunge whites and middle-class blacks from the school system," said Bolick, the institute's litigation director.

Desegregation Trials

In 1987, a federal court declared Boston sufficiently integrated to allow court-ordered busing to end.

City officials in 1989 went to a "controlled choice system," which allowed students to choose among 27 schools in their home zone as long as the choice of assignment would maintain a certain level of racial balance.

With race not a factor in determining school assignment and the apparent push to send city students to neighborhood schools, some experts see resegregation as a certainty, particularly if avoiding lawsuits is a school district's primary focus.

"Dropping desegregation altogether is a major mistake," said Gary Orfield, Harvard University professor of education and social policy. "The ultimate logic here, if conservatives have their way, is that any integration will be incidental, and anything planned, illegal."

Georgia School Accepts Race-Neutral Transfers

A Georgia school district in December 1999 ended its controversial forced busing program, approving an alternative method that doesn't take race into consideration when assigning students to schools.
The 7-0 vote of the DeKalb County School Board halts a program that barred student transfers if the result disturbed a school's racial balance.

The new program, to take effect this fall, allows any student in an overcrowded school to apply to another school with open seats, and race will not be a factor in reviewing the request.

About 4,000 elementary and middle students who are now bused will be permitted to attend their current school until they reach the highest grade level offered. The board's action averts a lawsuit from the Southeastern Legal Foundation, which threatened to sue the district if it forced currently enrolled students to remain in the transfer program until they graduated from high school.

North Carolina School Board Votes To Appeal End of Busing

The Charlotte-Mecklenburg Board of Education voted last October to appeal a September federal appeals court decision that ended a decades-old desegregation order.

In a divided decision on Oct. 6, 1999, the board also voted to ask U.S. District Court Judge Robert Potter to delay the effect of his Sept. 9 decision pending the results of the appeal to be filed shortly in *Swann v. Charlotte-Mecklenburg Board of Education* (97-CV-482).

Potter's ruling declared the school district "unitary," a legal term meaning that integration efforts in the previously segregated system have been successful and court oversight is no longer necessary.

The school district was ordered to stop assigning children to schools or allocating educational opportunities through busing, race-based lotteries, preferences, set-asides or means that do not afford students equal opportunities.

The board's majority favored appealing the ruling and asking for the injunction because it argued that Potter's decision hinders the district's attempts to remedy ongoing inequities between the predominantly white, suburban schools and the predominantly black, inner-city schools.

CHAPTER 2

Dress Codes

School officials in recent years have been grappling with how to accommodate students' increasingly individualistic fashion sense—while keeping order in the schoolhouse.

In an effort to limit belly-bearing midriffs, over-sized clothing and gang symbols, many districts across the country have instituted student dress codes, and some have gone a step further and adopted school uniforms.

But crafting dress codes that don't illegally trump First Amendment rights can be challenging, especially amid a socially diverse student body that, on any given day, might don pentagrams, Confederate flags, florescent hair colors, cross-dressing apparel, or just plain too *little* apparel.

And last year's school shooting spree in Littleton, Colo.. by members of the Trench Coat Mafia, so named because its student members wore long, dark trench coats, started a national discussion on the need to more closely monitor what students are wearing to school.

Although federal courts extend schools a great deal of latitude on what goes on within their boundaries, court rulings on the issue are not consistent, with some upholding aspects of dress codes and others invalidating them.

Sometimes school officials, faced with youth's propensity for the original and the bizarre, throw up their hands. For example, a Florida boy initially was barred from his school prom because he wanted to show up in a red evening gown and red shoes, fully accessorized with rhinestone jewelry.

After initially denying his request to show up in drag, school officials and attorneys changed their minds to avert a lawsuit.

Court rulings on the issue aren't consistent, in spite of landmark cases that allow school officials to limit speech or articles worn by students that might disrupt instruction, according to legal experts.

"First Amendment protections are the greatest when actual words are involved," said Leslie Stellman, an attorney who spoke at a recent Education Law Association conference.

She points to another example of how students tested the legal bounds of their rights. Massachusetts students in the early 1990s parodied their school's student dress code by wearing t-shirts with various slogans, such as "naked coeds." A federal district court in *Pyle v. South Hadley School Committee* (861 F. Supp. 157, 94 Ed. Law Rep. 729; D. Mass. 1994) ruled that a school could prohibit vulgar slogans on clothing.

In an opposite opinion, a state court on the same case used a 1969 U.S. Supreme Court ruling to determine that students can, under the First Amendment, wear clothing bearing vulgar slogans to school, as long as they do not disrupt school instruction.

But what constitutes a school disruption can be a matter of opinion— and a changing one at that.

For example, a Michigan school district amended its dress code to allow students to wear pentagrams after having classified the articles among a number of banned cultic or satanic articles.

The student, who professed to be a witch practicing the earth-based religion known as "white witchcraft" or Wicca, ultimately spurred a change in school policy on what is disruptive.

Three landmark cases are used to guide the domain of students' free speech rights, including dress codes or uniforms, though the degree to which the cases are applied varies greatly by the facts of individual cases:

- *Tinker v. Des Moines Community Independent School District* (393 U.S. 503, 1969): the U.S. Supreme Court affirms students' freedom of expression so long as they do "not engage in a type of expression that materially and substantially interferes with school-work or discipline;

- *Bethel School District No. 403 v. Fraser* (478 U.S. 675, 32 Ed. Law Rep. 1243, 1986): the high court rules that school districts can limit suggestive speech by students without violating their First Amendment rights.

- *Hazelwood School District v. Kuhlmeier* (108 S. Ct. 562, 1988): the Supreme Court affirmed school officials' right to control the content of student speech in school-sponsored activities, so long as the action is tied to an academic purpose.

Legal experts are predicting an erosion of the pro-student legal standard set in *Tinker* in the wake of escalating incidents of school violence. However, they also predict that courts will continue to protect the free speech rights of students who wish to express political or religious beliefs through dress.

SYMBOLS

Michigan Student Witch Wins Right To Wear Pentagram

A Michigan student who professes to be a witch won the right last year to wear a pentagram in school as a symbol of her faith.

School attorneys signed a consent decree to amend the anti-gang and anti-cult policy at Detroit's Lincoln Park High School to allow Crystal Seifferly, 17, an honor student, to wear the five-pointed star symbolic of her Wiccan religion to school.

The policy, announced in October 1998, banned any student from wearing pentagrams and clothing or symbols of Satanists, the Ku Klux Klan, skinheads, gangs, white supremacists or gothic dress of any kind. It called for the items to be confiscated and the student suspended indefinitely.

The American Civil Liberties Union sued the district in February 1999, saying the policy violated a student's rights by preventing her from wearing the symbol of her pagan faith. Wicca, whose members refer to themselves as witches, is a religion that celebrates seasonal and life cycles using rituals from pre-Christian Europe. Seifferly said her suit was not intended to spread her beliefs, but rather to preserve her constitutional right to display a symbol of her faith as openly as Christians or Jews.

She succeeded in forcing the school district to remove pagans and witches from the lists of groups "not appropriate to the school setting."

School attorneys said the policy aimed to make the school safer by suppressing the influence of a rising number of cults and other groups. They said it was not the policy's intention to ban religious symbols and it now is more specific on what symbols are acceptable.

Crystal said she continued to wear the pentagram after the policy was initiated but hid it under her shirt. Though the March 1999 settlement does not include monetary damages, the district agreed to pay $14,000 for Crystal's legal bills.

In Indiana, Hair Color Sidelines High School Cheerleader

An Indiana high school student was taken off the cheerleading squad earlier this year because school officials object to the hue of the natural blonde's newly dyed hair.

Sheridan High School officials say it's purple. She says it's a deep red— "True Red," according to the box of Nutrisse hair color she bought from a local Wal-Mart.

Sixteen-year-old Erin Godby, who has been a cheerleader since third grade, was suspended because officials say her hair color does not "meet a community standard we felt would be representative of Sheridan High School."

The high school sophomore concedes her hair didn't turn out as she expected. "It turned out a deep shade of red, but I don't see how you could call it purple," she told *The Indianapolis Star*.

But top school officials, alerted to her hair color by athletic director Larry Wright, thought it looked purple and suspended her after she refused to recolor it, maintaining that it is a dark red and not offensive. Erin and her mother also point to school rules for cheerleaders and the cheerleading contract Erin signed at the start of the season.

Neither mention regulations on hair color, they said. The only reference to hair involves length, for safety reasons, they said.

Now, Erin and her mother are talking to the American Civil Liberties Union and an attorney about a possible legal complaint.

John Krull of the Indiana ACLU said school officials should have greater concerns than "humiliating a young girl simply because a dye job went bad."

Brenda Godby, Erin's mother, said, "I've got a phone call in to an attorney about it, and I'm not sure what action we're going to take."

Erin is not the first student suspended over hair color. A Virginia boy was suspended indefinitely last year until he re-dyed his hair an "acceptable" color.

Suspension over Confederate Flag Violates Free Speech

Florida school officials who suspended a student for displaying a Confederate flag during an informal lunchtime discussion with friends violated his First Amendment rights, a federal appeals court has ruled.

Pine Ridge High School student Wayne Denno was speaking quietly with friends during lunch on Dec. 13, 1995, when he was approached by an administrator for holding a Confederate flag. Denno was telling his friends about his interest in Civil War reenactments and living histories.

When Assistant Principal Dennis Roberts ordered the student to put the flag away, Denno tried to explain to him the historical significance of the flag. Roberts then escorted Denno to an administrative office, where he was ultimately suspended. Denno later sued, alleging that the suspension violated his First Amendment rights to free speech.

"Given the alleged context of Denno's small group discussion—a small, quiet and confined discussion amongst Denno and his friends of Civil

War history and Denno's hobby as a Civil War reenactor—and given the alleged absence of any disruption or racial tension at the school, we conclude that Denno ... has alleged a violation of [his] First Amendment rights," wrote 11th Circuit Judge R. Lanier Anderson III for the 2-1 majority in July 1999.

Tinker Talk

Anderson used the landmark Supreme Court student rights' case *Tinker v. Des Moines Independent Community School District* (393 U.S. 503, 89 S. Ct. 733; 1969) to overrule part of a lower court decision in favor of the School Board of Volusia County, Fla.

"*Tinker* clearly establishes the law: a student has a right to display a symbol which, although it might reflect an unpopular viewpoint and evoke discomfort and unpleasantness, reasonably gives rise to nothing greater than an undifferentiated fear or apprehension of disturbance," Anderson wrote.

He did note that under *Tinker*, school officials may legally prohibit the display of symbols in circumstances that warrant "reasonable fear" those symbols would be disruptive to school discipline. However, Anderson wrote, there was no evidence of such a threat in *Denno v. School Board of Volusia County, Florida* (98-2718).

But Anderson agreed with the lower court that Denno could not sue the school district over his suspension because the district may only be held liable in these cases if there is an official policy banning displays that result in violations of the First Amendment.

Judge Susan Black dissented from the majority, disagreeing with its *Tinker* argument and rejecting the idea that school officials violated Denno's First Amendment rights. The school is "a racially integrated school in the Deep South," she wrote.

Nothing in this case establishes the "unreasonableness of a school official's belief that the display of a Confederate battle flag ... might lead to a material disruption." The appeals court sent the case back to the lower court for review in light of the ruling.

ATTIRE

Florida School Officials Let Boy Wear Dress to Prom

The senior prom wasn't a black-tie affair for one Florida teenage boy who convinced school officials to allow him to show up in drag. Officials at Taylor High School in Pierson, Fla., had told senior Charles Rice that he would be stopped at the door if he showed up in a dress.

The 18-year-old eventually wore a red evening gown, red satin shoes, gloves and matching rhinestone jewelry to the 1999 prom. Rice, who is gay, said he just wanted the right to "express himself."

Although Principal Peter Oatman told Rice two weeks before the prom that he could not show up in drag, Oatman changed his mind after conferring with Superintendent Bill Hall and school attorneys and reviewing news accounts of his decision.

Hall said officials reversed their decision only because the principal had let Rice wear skirts and dresses to special events in the past, and that would have weakened the school's case had the student sued.

Texas School Board Upholds Suspension over Belt Buckle

A Jasper school board affirmed the decision of a middle school principal to suspend a 14-year old for repeatedly donning a Confederate belt buckle.

The board voted in March 1999 to uphold the principal's action against Josh Letney, who was suspended from Jasper Middle School because he refused school officials' requests to remove the buckle. It violates the school's dress code regulations because the buckle could cause disruption.

Gwen Gilford, the school's principal, asked Josh not to wear the belt buckle to school in reverence to the dragging death last June of Jasper resident James Byrd Jr.

John William King, a self-described white supremacist, has been convicted and sentenced to death for the crime.

While school officials consider the belt buckle a violation of the school's dress code, Josh insists that the buckle, a gift from his uncle, represents his heritage and Southern roots.

A federal court in a Kansas case ruled against a boy who tried to overturn his suspension for drawing a Confederate flag in school, arguing that public school students don't have the same rights as adults when exercising their First Amendment rights results in class disruption.

CHAPTER 3

Faculty Employment

Whether the issue is free speech, freedom of religion, age discrimination or affirmative action, hiring and firing policies at schools and institutions of higher learning have grown increasingly complex. For example:

- A federal court in Michigan ordered a community college to reinstate a professor suspended for using profane language in the classroom.

- A North Carolina Wiccan teacher alleged that school officials suspended her for being a witch, but then she ultimately resigned.

- The nation's top court shielded state colleges and universities from federal age-discrimination lawsuits filed by older employers.

Achieving and retaining order among faculty members—setting policy on speech, religion, disciplinary issues and hiring and firing—without stepping on their civil rights is partly a matter of carefully reviewing the laws governing this realm of employment, partly a matter of common sense.

In the area of faculty speech, generally two U.S. Supreme Court cases govern the domain of free speech for public employees: *Pickering v. Board of Education* (391 U.S. 563, 8 S. Ct. 173; 1968) and *Connick v. Myers* (461 U.S. 138, 103 S. Ct. 1731;1983).

These two cases comprise the two-part test used to determine whether speech by public employees, or in this case, faculty, is constitutionally protected.

First, *Connick* establishes that it must be determined whether the faculty member's speech is a matter of public interest. Specifically, that interest must involve "political, social, or other concern to the community." Impacting that determination is a review of the content, delivery and context of a statement, the ruling says. If the speech is not a matter of public interest, the courts will not consider the firing or other disciplinary action—"absent the most unusual circumstances"—illegal.

But if the speech is a matter of public concern, a standard set by *Pickering* applies, which essentially balances the interest of the employee "as a citizen, in commenting upon matters of public interest and the interest of the State, as an employer, in promoting the efficiency of the public service it performs through its employees."

As is often the case, determining how to respond without incurring liability is not an easy task, and the legal results are sometimes uncertain.

That is what Macomb Community College discovered when a federal court ordered it to reinstate a professor it suspended for using sexually explicit language in the classroom. The teacher publicly denounced the school's disciplinary action in a lengthy memo.

The professor won, at least the first round, when the court granted him a temporary injunction, giving him his job back pending litigation.

But the teachers aren't always the winners in these cases, as an Oklahoma teacher and a Wiccan teacher from North Carolina might attest to. The Wiccan teacher originally accused school officials of suspending her for being a practicing witch, violating her rights to freedom of religion. Ultimately, she ended up resigning after a media firestorm and signing an agreement with the school district.

A federal appeals court allowed an Oklahoma school district to fire a teacher for breaching student privacy rules after he intimidated a male student who reported him for making lewd comments about female anatomy.

Federal circuits typically apply their own standard of review to these cases. Legal experts recommend the following:

- Investigate the incident.

- Determine how the employee's speech has impaired or disrupted the operation of the institution.

- Determine whether the conduct—as a broader issue than the speech alone—is a valid basis of discipline.

* * *

Age discrimination gained much attention this term with the U.S. Supreme Court's decision in *Kimel v. Florida Board of Regents* (98-791) and *MacPherson et al. v. University of Montevallo* (96-6947). In a consolidated ruling, the high court made it more difficult for older employees to file lawsuits when they say their rights have been violated.

Employees have generally had a tough time trying to garner sympathetic rulings from federal courts under the Age Discrimination in Employment Act, which forbids employers from firing their workers based solely on age.

* * *

Affirmative action in employment rightly has been a major concern of school officials, since the issue has been a significant source of lawsuits against school districts in recent years.

The issue has come under increasing attack, with some courts ruling in favor of schools' diversity efforts; federal court rulings of late have not been favorable for the use of race at public institutions.

The U.S. Supreme Court refused to hear arguments in a 1998 Nevada case in which a federal court allowed a university to pay a black professor more than a white one.

At the secondary-school level, the high court almost heard arguments in a New Jersey case in which a white teacher sued her school district for racial discrimination, after the board laid her off and retained a black instructor. But the school district moved to settle the case before it became the basis of national legal precedent. The teacher received a large sum of money.

* * *

But perhaps the most volatile issue facing faculty employment is how to better screen school staff, often charged with educating the most impressionable and vulnerable of students.

"Increasingly, parents and taxpayers have demanded accountability for the actions of school personnel in screening prospective employees," said A. Dean Picket, an attorney with the law firm of Magnum, Wall, Stoops & Warden.

"Courts have recognized both the right and the responsibility of school districts to investigate the backgrounds of candidates for employment," he said at a school law conference last year.

States have moved to mandate better background checks for schools. And federal courts are encouraging such efforts by ruling in favor of school districts conducting such background and holding liable those that fail to do so.

For example, the Fifth Circuit ruled that "the right to hold public employment is not a recognized fundamental right," and school boards do not violate the civil rights of applicants with felony convictions by conducting investigations.

"Looking a little deeper into a convicted felon's background and, in particular, at the circumstances of the conviction is rationally related to serve the legitimate interest in protecting the school children within that teacher's proximity and care," the court ruled in *Hillary v. Ferguson* (30 F.3d 649, 652; 1994). The Fifth Circuit court used a 1976 case of *Massachusetts Board of Retirement v. Margi* (427 U.S. 307, 313) as the basis for its decision.

In a second case, *Marcy v. Neo* (662 A.2d 272; 1995), a federal court in New Hampshire ruled that school districts have a responsibility not to hire school employees they know, or should know, have a tendency to sexually abuse students.

One school attorney said at a law conference that the real issue here is "not avoiding liability, but avoiding injury to children."

Either way, the task of hiring, firing or setting policy governing employees comes with no guarantee that litigation won't ensue.

HIRING/TENURE

Supreme Court Turns Away Georgia Tenure Case

The U.S. Supreme Court last year refused to review a case in which a Georgia professor accused a university of denying her tenure on the basis of age and sex.

Lower courts were split on the issue of whether a faculty member is entitled to tenure by virtue of her years of service and the completion of the probationary-period requirement established by an institution's written tenure policies.

The 11th Circuit Court of Appeals last August upheld a district court ruling that dismissed a lawsuit filed by former assistant professor Jill Gray against the University of Georgia. She accused the school of violating her rights under Title VII of the 1964 Civil Rights Act, the Age Discrimination in Employment Act and the 14th Amendment.

Title VII bars employers from discriminating on the basis of sex, race, color or religion. The 14th Amendment ensures the right to due process.

But the university asserted 11th Amendment immunity from Gray's suit. The 11th Amendment protects the government from being sued except when its agents are found to have committed gross acts of negligence.

The university also said Gray's nine-year stint as a mathematics teacher was "pursuant to a series of one-year contracts until her non-renewal, which followed her failure to complete successfully the Board of Regents' formal tenure review process."

Gray's attorneys, however, said she was given no formal reason for being denied tenure, despite following the direction of officials to obtain advanced degrees to increase her chances of being awarded tenure. They argued that her advanced work and the fact that she met the probationary period necessary to qualify for tenure should have secured her job and tenure, not resulted in a dismissal.

The high court refused to review *Gray v. Board of Regents of the University System of Georgia* (98-1246) without comment.

18-Year-Olds Too Young To Drive School Buses, Court Rules

A Louisiana appeals court in July 1999 agreed with a school board's decision not to hire an 18-year-old who sought a job as a school bus driver.

"It is a legitimate interest of the government to set standards of experience required of a school bus driver," wrote Judge Jimmie Peters of the Third Circuit Court of Appeals for Louisiana.

"By the very act of requiring a five-year background driving record check of an applicant, the law eliminates 18-year-old drivers, as they can only have two years of experience since a valid driver's license cannot be obtained until someone reaches 16 years of age," wrote Peters in the majority opinion in *Demars v. Natchitoches Parish School Board* (98-1963).

When Monte Demars graduated from Lakeview High School in Natchitoches Parish in May 1995, he told staffers in the transportation department that he wanted to become a bus driver.

He completed a 40-hour bus driver's instructional program and obtained a commercial driver's license from the Louisiana Department of Public Safety. But after he met those requirements, the school board rejected his application based on age restrictions set by state laws.

The Natchitoches school superintendent sought a waiver of the age limitation from the state for Demars, but the state refused. Demars sued, arguing that the provision is discriminatory and unconstitutional, and is in conflict with another statute that appears to allow exceptions for the 21-years-of-age requirement for college bus drivers.

A trial court found that the two statutes do not conflict. It held that they serve different purposes—one applies to drivers of school-age children and the other to college-age students—but the provisions are constitutional. The court rejected Demars' request for damages.

FIRING

Federal Court Favors Oklahoma School District in Teacher Firing

A federal appeals court last year upheld an Oklahoma school board's firing of a teacher who allegedly breached student privacy rules and made suggestive comments to students.

Stephen P. Harjo worked for Varnum Public Schools until April 1997, when school officials fired him for intimidating a male student to whom he reportedly made lewd remarks about female anatomy, and for criticizing the teacher who reported him to superiors.

Harjo—who had been at the school for one year—sued the district, saying he was denied due process and the opportunity to improve his performance and clear his name.

A three-judge panel of the U.S. 10th District Court of Appeals affirmed a lower court ruling in favor of the school district.

Harjo "received all of the process to which he was due, including a full-blown hearing at which he had the opportunity to clear his name," wrote 10th District Judge Bobby R. Baldock in *Harjo v. Varnum* (98-7023).

Harjo's complaint is based on the outcome of the hearing, not the procedures used to set it up, the ruling went on to say. He did not dispute the facts of the charges against him or prove that the hearing was biased, partial or unfair, the ruling stated.

10th Circuit Upholds Age Discrimination Verdict

The 10th Circuit Court of Appeals ruled that the dismissal of a 55-year-old principal did not constitute age discrimination.

Carlton Allen, former chief at Caney Valley High School in Kansas, claimed that the decision of the school board and superintendent not to renew his contract violated the Age Discrimination in Employment Act (ADEA).

Allen argued that the school board fired him because he was one year away from receiving his early retirement benefits and then replaced him with a younger man to fill his job—a text book example of age discrimination.

ADEA prohibits employers from firing their workers based solely on age. If age is a factor in dismissing an employee, the employer must show other reasons for firing the employee

The 10th Circuit upheld a federal district court of Kansas ruling in *Carlton Allen v. Board of Education* (93-1321) that Allen was fired because of his poor performance, not because he was old. Furthermore, the appeals court upheld the lower court's ruling that eligibility for retirement is not evidence of age discrimination.

End of a Saga

The appeals court's decision ends a long chapter in Kansas education law.

In the early 90s, the Kansas courts were split on whether principals had the right to a fair review from their school boards before they were fired. In addition to the age-discrimination case, Allen filed a complaint in state court charging that the school board conspired to interfere with his contract. The state appeals court initially ruled that Allen deserved a review hearing before he was canned.

This decision, however, was overturned when the Kansas Supreme Court ruled in *Brown v. USD* that principals do not have the same rights as other public employees; for instance, they don't have a right to long-term contracts, the way teachers do.

"For our teacher members who were part of the suit, we are glad this is finally over with," said Marjorie Blauhuss, staff attorney for the Kansas National Education Association.

California Court Helps Teachers Who Are Fighting Dismissals

Tenured public school teachers may find it easier to challenge dismissals or suspensions following a California Supreme Court ruling that protects them from financial liability if they lose.

Ruling it unconstitutional, the state high court in May 1999 overturned a state law that required teachers who fight disciplinary actions and lose to pay half the cost of a state administrative hearing.

The 4-3 ruling in *California Teachers Association v. State of California* (SO67030) found that the law violated teachers' due process rights under the Constitution because it discouraged them from acting on their legal right to challenge suspensions or dismissals.

In the majority ruling written by Chief Justice Ronald George, the court ruled that the 1976 state law discourages teachers from fighting disciplinary action "by making it expensive to do so." The law makes teachers vulnerable to "baseless charges" that may never be challenged "simply because the teacher fears incurring liability for the [hearing] cost," he wrote.

But Justice Kathryn Mickle Werdagar led the dissent in arguing that the law already offers tenured teachers "substantial protection."

North Carolina Wiccan Teacher Resigns after Media Firestorm

A North Carolina teacher suspended after school officials discovered she is a practicing witch resigned from her job in January 2000, calling it the "best thing" for her students.

Shari Eicher, who practices a nature-centered religion known as Wicca, issued a joint statement with the Scotland County Board of Education that her "effectiveness in the classroom has been undermined at the present time by media and community attention."

"This was the best thing for my students," she said. "The best thing I can say is, it's over."

The Jan. 27 statement asserts that the school district has not trumped Eicher's civil rights, including her freedom of religion rights.

It makes clear that the 11th-grade teacher has not tried to convert any of her students, colleagues or others in the community to Wicca, also known as white witchcraft. A major tenant of this religion is to cause no harm, since one's actions will yield three times the blessing or curse.

Eicher was suspended from Scotland County High School with pay on Jan. 10. Eicher and her husband, Richard, are both ordained Wiccan ministers and members of a small coven called WillowFyre. They said most Wiccans focus on positive energy.

There was no information on whether a monetary award was included in the agreement between Eicher and school officials.

The Eichers have said they suspect some residents of Scotland County started a debate about their religion after viewing their Web site, which is no longer posted.

AFFIRMATIVE ACTION

Affirmative Action Scores a Win in Boston Schools

A Boston jury in February threw out the case of a white teacher who claimed the city school system passed her over in favor of less qualified minority candidates.

The Feb. 14 dismissal by a Suffolk Superior Court jury was a key win for Boston city schools' affirmative action efforts.

The case, filed by elementary art teacher Elizabeth Joseph, could have dismantled the last remnant of affirmative action in Boston's schools by forcing officials to end historic efforts to maintain racial balance in their teaching staff.

Boston school officials expressed relief.

"We're delighted with the jury's finding that there was no form of racial or age discrimination here," Boston School Superintendent Thomas Payzant said. "This is a strong decision that affirms the necessity of allowing local school districts, while meeting a standard of fairness, to recruit and select the most qualified teachers they can find."

Joseph did not comment, but her attorney, Paul Nevins, said they are considering an appeal.

The lawsuit took aim at the 25-year-old federal order of U.S. District Court Judge W. Arthur Garrity Jr., which ordered Boston schools to desegregate and set aside 20 percent of teaching slots for black teachers and 10 percent for Hispanic or other minority instructors.

Nevins presented evidence that 36 minority teachers hired before Joseph for art or music positions lacked state certification or required a state waiver in order to teach without one.

He argued that Joseph, who is certified, was denied a job for more than six years because of affirmative action.

Boston officials eventually hired Joseph, who now teaches at the city's Josiah Quincy School. City officials would have had to pay her hundreds of thousands of dollars in back pay and emotional damages had the jury ruled in her favor.

Nevins said it was difficult to demonstrate Joseph's qualifications as a better teacher without observing her teaching style. But "we fought hard," he said. "It's hard to say what is in the minds of the jury."

City officials said they are dedicated to maintaining the progress made under the desegregation efforts of the last three decades.

For example, roughly 30 years ago, minorities made up 5 percent of the teachers in city schools and 39 percent of the students. Now, 85 percent of the students and 39 percent of the teachers are minorities.

If Joseph decides to appeal, the odds could be in her favor. Across the country, federal and state courts have been ruling in favor of white plaintiffs in education-related affirmative action cases. As a result, some school systems are backing away from race-based policies and moving to color-blind admissions systems.

Race Case Fizzled before High Court Heard It

Affirmative action in hiring, which started as one of the most far-reaching education issues to hit the U.S. Supreme Court in years, was yanked off the docket in a last-minute settlement.

But the issue didn't die there: lower courts throughout the United States continue to grapple with the issue.

The High Court in August 1998 was poised to hear arguments from a white teacher who said she was the victim of racial discrimination because of a New Jersey school board's decision to lay her off and retain a black instructor.

Using money raised from civil rights groups, the school board agreed to pay $433,500 to Sharon Taxman, who claimed her civil rights were violated when she was dismissed in May 1989.

In *Board of Education of Piscataway v. Taxman* (96-679), some liberal groups had feared the Court's increasing hostility toward affirmative action could have ended the practice nationwide.

It Ain't Dead Yet

The Supreme Court's 1979 decision in *Regents of the University of California v. Bakke* (438 U.S. 265) determined that schools can use race as a factor in admissions *(see Chapter 1: Affirmative Action)*.

The concept, however, has come under attack at universities in Texas, California, Washington and Michigan.

U.S. district and circuit courts are diluting *Bakke* by placing limits on affirmative action, said William Taylor, a Washington, D.C., civil rights attorney.

The U.S. Fifth Circuit Court of Appeals, in *Texas v. Hopwood* (95-1773) for example, supported a narrow interpretation of Bakke, saying race could be considered in efforts to remove bias at schools, but not society at large. The Supreme Court turned away Hopwood and let the Fifth Circuit ruling stand.

"The Hopwood decision absolutely ruled out diversity as a rationale," Taylor said. "It was an improper decision."

"I think the dilemma for advocates of affirmative action is that the case law is being eroded by the lower courts," Taylor added.

Taylor said "the buzz" among school lawyers is to eliminate race-conscious decisions for student programs. "Lawyers are advising school boards not to be race-conscious," he said.

High Court Retains Ruling in Reverse Job Bias Case

The U.S. Supreme Court in March 1998 left intact a Nevada court's decision that allowed a university to pay a black faculty member more than a white instructor to foster staff diversity.

The justices, without comment, refused to review the affirmative action case at the University of Nevada at Reno (UNR) that some observers hoped would provide a definitive ruling from the conservative Court on race and gender preferences.

"I'm sure this will come as a surprise and relief to national civil rights groups," said attorney David Rubin, who represented a New Jersey school district in an affirmative action case that was settled last year when black leaders raised money to avoid a High Court decision.

But civil rights attorney William Taylor of Washington, D.C., said the High Court's action only means "they're not rushing in at the moment to totally revamp the rules on affirmative action."

Super-Size Faculty?

The suit in Nevada was filed under Title VII of the 1964 Civil Rights Act, which bars employers from discriminating based on race or national origin.

While two federal appeals courts have ruled recently that schools can use race as a factor only to remedy past discrimination, the Nevada state supreme court ruled in *Farmer v. University of Nevada* (930 P.2d 730) that Title VII also allows schools to use race in employment decisions to promote diversity.

In 1990, UNR adopted an unwritten "minority bonus" preference policy allowing each department to hire an additional faculty member for every minority hired. Yvette Farmer, a white female, and Johnson Makoba, a black male, applied for an opening in the sociology department.

University guidelines require departments to interview more than one candidate, but the sociology department got a waiver to interview only Makoba. He was hired at a starting salary of $35,000, with a $5,000 increase after completion of his dissertation.

One year later, under the bonus policy, UNR hired Farmer as the additional faculty member.

But she received a starting salary of $31,000, plus a $2,000 increase after finishing her dissertation. The salary difference between the two instructors widened to $10,838.

Farmer sued the university under Title VII and the Equal Pay Act. A jury awarded her $40,000, but Nevada's supreme court reversed the ruling.

The state court ruled that, because UNR's faculty was about 88 percent white and only 1 percent black, its minority preference policy was trying to attain racial balance and didn't unnecessarily harm white employees.

Comparing Bakke

The judges cited the 1979 High Court decision in *Regents of the University of California v. Bakke* (438 U.S. 265), which said schools can use race as a factor in admissions. The Nevada court said UNR had a "compelling interest" in achieving a racially diverse faculty.

"A failure to attract minority faculty perpetuates the university's white enclave and further limits student exposure to multicultural diversity," the state court said.

The ruling contrasts with a 1996 decision by the U.S. Third Circuit Court of Appeals in *Piscataway Board of Education v. Taxman* (91 F.3d 1547). In that case, judges said Title VII did not allow a school district to lay off a white teacher and retain a black teacher to promote diversity.

Matching White Landscapes

Farmer's attorney, Sharon Browne, told the High Court in a brief that the racial composition of UNR's faculty was "nearly a mirror image" of the surrounding population. The city of Reno and the state of Nevada's white population were 86 percent and 88 percent, respectively.

"The university paid a white female professor significantly less than a black male professor, and the [Nevada] court validated this dual pay scale," Browne said in her brief. "Under this reasoning, the perceived need for racial diversity ... becomes an absolute defense" to discrimination suits.

Eugene Volokh, professor at the UCLA School of Law, said Farmer presented the Court with unusual facts because the female faculty member was hired and was being paid a normal pay scale. But he said the Court will have more opportunities to define Title VII.

"This issue still isn't resolved — when can the government discriminate against whites and males?" Volokh said.

Browne said the Court's action didn't swing the pendulum in favor of affirmative action again.

"I would not encourage any public employer to read anything into *Farmer* to use race to diversify faculty," Browne said.

CHAPTER 4

Freedom of Speech

If the computer has done more to transform the classroom than any other technological advancement of the 20th Century, then the rush to "get wired" has brought with it a need for school officials to ponder how to limit the dangers of students surfing the Internet.

An innocent search for "toys," for example, may link students to sexually explicit Web sites. But Internet blocking software designed to prevent students from accessing certain words may impede students' legitimate study of cities such as "Middlesex" or human anatomy.

General chat rooms, which many school districts ban students from accessing, pose another set of dangers with the potential of exposing children to deviants or criminals.

But amid the complications of providing Internet access are computer-savvy students who, under the guise of freedom of speech, may push the bar on what school officials consider acceptable use of a computer at home or school.

It has grown common in recent years: Students using the Internet at school and home to make threats, or for what is commonly called "hate speech" directed at other students, teachers and the administration in general.

"The core question is whether such acts fall within the scope of the district's disciplinary policy, or whether First Amendment free speech rights trump any punishment that might otherwise be applied," said Edwin Darden, a staff attorney at the National School Boards Association. He was one of several school attorneys and administrators addressing this issue at a recent conference.

There are no clear legal standards in this area, Darden says, because "the proliferation of technology use by students inside and outside school has generated a host of new legal dilemmas that must be untangled by the courts."

The electronic highway has collided with what used to be reasonably clear-cut legal standards on school officials' authority to curtail on-campus speech. Three Supreme Court cases generally form the legal basis for that authority:

1. *Tinker v. Des Moines Independent School District* (393 U.S. 503, 89 S. Ct. 733, 21 L.Ed. 2d 731;1969) affirmed students' First Amendment right to engage in non-disruptive demonstration on school grounds unless it can be proven that the action causes, or would cause, both a "material" and a "substantial" disruption of school routine.

2. *Bethel School District v. Fraser* (478 U.S. 675, 106 S. Ct. 3159, 92 L.Ed. 2d 549; 1986) held that the First Amendment does not trump the rights of school officials to discipline students for lewd or indecent speeches.

3. *Hazelwood School District v. Kulmeier* (484 U.S. 260, 108 S. Ct. 562, 98 L.Ed.2d 592; 1988) established school officials' right to control the content of student speech in school-sponsored activities, as long as the censorship is reasonably tied to an educational purpose.

Darden also pointed to a 1997 case, *Reno v. ACLU* (117 S. Ct. 2329), which gave students the right to speak freely on the Internet, deemed a public marketplace of ideas.

What blurs the line between what is within school officials' authority and what is not is the manner in which personal use of Internet technology narrows the distance between home and school.

"With an electronic highway as the link, the two locales can be virtually seamless and the impact of home-based keyboarding can have a profound effect on the safety, security and orderliness of the school environment," Darden said.

For example, in 1998 a Fairfax County, Va., high school student professing to be a Satanist posted a list of about 12 people on his Website, threatening that he would kill them once he "snapped."

School officials contacted Fairfax County police, who investigated the case, but ultimately did not press charges because the boy did not transmit the list to others. School officials did suspend the boy for the rest of that school year. But because police found that he did not use a school computer to create the Website, school officials opted not to expel him, the more common punishment for students who write such "hit lists" in the county.

Fairfax County school policy calls for the suspension and possibly expulsion of students who make such threats against students or teachers.

Darden gives another example:

An 11th grade honor student from King George County, Va., posted a Web site on which he threatened to kidnap and rape a coach. The boy also threatened other teachers and students on his site. Near the names he wrote: "If you're on here, you may find yourself rolled up in a carpet and headed for the bridge."

Darden said the uncertainty of the law caused school officials to decide not to act, instead allowing law enforcement to investigate any violation of law. The student dismantled the Web site when the controversy hit.

Like police and prosecutors in Fairfax County, King George prosecutors completed their investigation without pressing charges because the boy didn't transit the threat to create a criminal offense.

The King George boy, after speaking with school officials, agreed to be punished and apologized, Darden said.

"Leaving the issue to police and prosecutors is a technique that may get school districts off the hook in declining to extend their discipline policy to off-campus Web speech," he said. "If the hate site is egregious enough or includes specific threats, there are at least two other potential avenues of redress."

In cases where the hate site is particularly threatening or severe, Darden noted that sometimes the teachers or students targeted by it may file a civil suit against the creator of the site.

In one case, an Indiana student who in August 1999 posted a Web site saying several school staff members are Satan worshipers; the staffers sued the boy's parents for money damages. The case is pending.

Of the multitude of cases involving students' inappropriate use of the Internet, none have set legal precedent, but as Darden and other legal experts note, school officials aren't eager to risk a costly lawsuit arising from students' discipline in this untested area.

For example, one Ohio student who was initially suspended from school for insulting his band teacher on his Web site ultimately received $30,000 and an apology from school officials in a settlement after a judge ruled in his favor during a preliminary ruling.

Sometimes it is not hate, but sexually explicit material posted on a Web site, that gets students into trouble. Take the case of the Washington high school senior who created a Web page allegedly as a parody of classmates' obsession with football and sex.

He included a link to *Playboy* magazine and stories about masturbation and oral sex. The student lost his school's endorsement for a National Merit Scholarship, and it rescinded its support of his enrollment in several colleges. The boy sued the school, which ultimately settled the case and allowed him to reapply for the scholarship. The school also paid him $2,000.

In this case, Darden explains school officials failed to give the student notice of the impending action and give him a hearing.

Another twist in this area occurs when students create links to schools' officials Web pages. When a Missouri high school senior created a Web page that used vulgar language to criticize teachers and administrators, and then linked it to his school's official home page, school officials suspended the boy for 10 days.

He removed the site and served the suspension, but then school officials said he had missed too many days from school and failed him in all of his classes, forcing him to graduate late. He sued, and a federal judge blocked the school's action pending the litigation.

School attorneys in the case argued that the student learned to create Web pages at the school, creating a connection between his action and the school setting. Students in the school's computer class read the site, creating another link—potential disruption—to the school environment.

Although this area of the law lacks clear legal guidance on how to handle these cases, some school districts may opt to approach these incidents as they do others involving off-campus offenses that have the potential to spill onto school grounds. In many school districts, officials hold students accountable for off-campus crimes or offenses.

But administrators may want consider these words from Darden: "This is an area that will continue to percolate and [evolve] as the number of incidents increase and the conflicts between teacher and students [escalate] into court cases.

"Most cases at this point are being settled before fully developing, leaving school officials and civil libertarians in a state of flux. It is hard to predict whether free speech or control of the school environment will ultimately prevail, and it may depend on the facts and circumstances of each case," Darden noted.

INTERNET MONITORING AND CONTENT

Schools Face Legal Risks As More Get on Internet

Schools should forge Internet contracts with students, parents, teachers and administrators to limit legal liability, experts say.

The contracts should be specific, but should include a "zipper clause," or catch-all statements, to cover infractions a schools' Internet policy committee didn't think of, Steve Permuth, a University of South Florida law professor, told members of the National Association of Elementary School Principals meeting last year in New Orleans.

Schools must approach Internet access with caution because so many legal issues still are unsettled, Permuth said.

For example, he said, the courts have yet to rule on whether Internet filtering programs in the school's violate the First Amendment's prohibition against censorship; a principal's liability for children exposed to obscene material on a school's computer; and the status of copyright laws as they pertain to the material on school Web sites.

"Principals need to diminish their vulnerability," Permuth said. They must remember they are "ultimately responsible, by site or area of concern, for the development of policies, rules and regulation for the appropriate conduct of the school."

Parental Consent

Schools should treat Internet access the same way they deal with school trips and get the parents to sign a permission slip. This protects against parents who may potentially sue a school for exposing their children to obscene material.

Schools should have the student sign an Internet usage agreement, laying out acceptable and unacceptable use for the Web and the consequences for breaking their terms.

Finally, parents need to sign these agreements to indicate that they understand that their children understand the contract between the student and the school; otherwise, the contracts will mean nothing legally.

Without such an agreement, the principal may be on the wrong end of an educational access lawsuit if a teacher takes away a student's Internet privileges. "Withdrawing education as a punishment is going to be looked at unfavorably if you don't present a good reason," Permuth said.

The Filter

One of the biggest questions for school administrators is whether to install an Internet filtering program along with their ISDN line and net-surfing software.

Last year, Sen. John McCain, R-Ariz., and Rep. Ernest Istook, R-Okla., attached legislation to appropriations bills that would have required schools to install such software if they benefited from federal Internet subsidies. Currently, McCain is holding a series of hearings on the issue to reopen the question.

Permuth, however, cautions against schools adopting Internet blocking software because it ultimately allows an entity other than the school to restrict content for its students.

In *Mainstream Loudon v. Board of Trustees of the Loudon County Library*, the U.S. District Court ruled that the library could not arbitrarily install filtering software in their computers because it was paramount to censorship. While public schools and libraries are treated much differently under the law, schools may run into a similar problem, depending on how the courts interpret two critical Supreme Court decisions in the student rights arena.

Permuth reasons that if the courts adopt the absolutist view of a student's right articulated in *Tinker v. Des Moines*—where the court upheld a student's right to wear an arm band in protest of the Vietnam War—then the filtering software won't be allowed unless unfiltered Internet use disrupts the school decorum.

This case says that students and teachers enjoy the same rights outside the schoolhouse as they do inside. Under the logic of *Tinker*, the filtering software would likely be seen as censorship, as it was in the Loudon library case.

But if the courts adopt the reasoning of the 1988 *Hazelwood School District v. Kuhlmeier* that upheld the right of school officials to edit a student publication, the filter software may be allowed.

Instead of taking the risk, Permuth recommends that schools adopt the same tack as the private sector when it comes to Internet usage, and let students know that they are being watched. "The emphasis should be on quality training programs of teachers and students, but not an emphasis on filtering and blocking," he said.

Permuth recommends that schools adopt Internet monitoring software so students know that if they click on a porn star's Website, their teacher will know about it, and that this will serve as a disincentive for such unwarranted surfing.

Los Angeles School Board Settles Software Copyright Suit

The Los Angeles Board of Education last year approved a $300,000 award to settle a lawsuit from a computer trade group that alleged the illegal use of copyrighted software programs in schools.

The settlement also requires the Los Angeles Unified School District to spend $1.5 million over the next three years for an eight-member team to investigate and stop any unauthorized duplication of computer software.

The group would be responsible for training school staff and students on the district's policy against illegally duplicating computer programs.

The suit, brought by an organization formed by Microsoft Corp., Novell Inc. and other computer software companies, charged the district's West Valley Occupational Center with using unauthorized copies of various types of software, such as Microsoft Word and Adobe Photoshop.

An investigation by the group uncovered more than 1,400 copies of software allegedly used without authorization. The group had asked for more than $562,000 in damages, and the cost to the school district, including setting up the task group, was expected to soar to $5 million.

Although district officials denied the accusation, school attorneys pressed the district to settle before a costly trial.

Industry experts said the Los Angeles suit may have brought to light the worst case of software piracy discovered in the U.S. education system.

Teachers Accused of Devil Worship on Web Sue Student

A student who posted a Web site suggesting that three teachers are devil worshippers will go to court to answer for his actions.

The teachers were named on Carmel High School student Brian Conradt's Web site. They filed suit last August in Hamilton County Circuit Court, in Noblesville, Ind., accusing the boy of defamation of character, intentional infliction of emotional distress and portraying the teachers in a "false light."

Brian allegedly created a Web site that included satanic symbols, such as a flaming pentagram. It reportedly also listed the names of 11 school district employees, including eight teachers at the high school. He questioned whether the teachers are "innocent teachers compelled to help others? Or are they really Satan worshipping demons?"

The site encouraged readers to tell the teachers that their "secret" had been exposed and to "laugh in their faces." An online nickname posted for the host was "tyme-2-dye."

"When I see students are instructed to confront me in the hallway, to shun me, and the person who put this up is called 'tyme-2-dye,' I take this as a threat," said plaintiff Diana Jill Grimes, a geography teacher at the Carmel, Ind., school.

"The suit is a way of saying, 'It's not right,'" she said. "A school should be a safe place. You shouldn't be scared to send your child to school. And I shouldn't be afraid to work."

The suit asks for $15,000 from Brian and his mother under an Indiana statute, mostly applied to vandalism cases, aimed at holding parents responsible for the destructive behavior of their children. The boy's mother, Laurie Hansen, said the suit is an overreaction to the site, which she said was meant as a joke. She said her son "feels very sorry and bad about this."

Judge Blocks Porn Law in Name of Free Speech

A federal judge in Philadelphia blocked a law that he said would have thwarted constitutionally protected free-speech rights in aiming to protect minors from sexually explicit Internet sites.

The Child Online Protection Act (COPA), which makes it a federal crime for commercial Web sites to communicate material considered "harmful to minors," was to take effect Feb. 1, 1999, when a temporary restraining order issued in November by U.S. District Judge Lowell Reed Jr. would have expired.

In *American Civil Liberties Union v. Janet Reno* (98-5591), Reed wrote, "[P]erhaps we do the minors of this country harm if First Amendment protections, which they will inherit fully, are chipped away in the name of their protection ...

"Despite the Court's personal regret that this preliminary injunction will delay once again the careful protection of our children, I without hesitation acknowledge ... the greater good."

The American Civil Liberties Union is leading the fight against the law, saying it amounts to "federal online censorship."

The ruling came after a six-day hearing in federal court at which Web site operators who provide free information about news, the fine arts, gay and lesbian issues, and sexual health for women and the disabled testified that the law would force them to shut down their Web sites.

"After listening to our clients describe their online speech, the court was clearly convinced that this new law would silence many voices on the Internet," said ACLU attorney Ann Beeson, lead counsel in the case, in a statement.

In the 49-page opinion, Reed said protecting minors is a compelling interest, but also said the law is still not effective because of minors' ability to gain access to other "harmful materials" on foreign Web sites, noncommercial sites and other Web-based sources.

The penalties for violating the law would include criminal and civil fines of up to $150,000 a day and up to six months in jail.

But Reed said the bigger issue is the "burden imposed on the protected speech, not the pressure placed on the pocketbooks or bottom lines of plaintiffs." COPA marks the second major attempt by Congress to protect children from accessing adult materials online.

The Communications Decency Act, which passed in 1996, was struck down as unconstitutional by the Supreme Court in 1997. The act outlawed making "indecent" material available to minors on the Internet.

RELIGION

SCHOOL PRAYER

High Court To Hear Texas Prayer Case

The U.S. Supreme Court on Nov. 15, 1999, agreed to review a Texas case that will determine whether student-led prayers at football games violate constitutional mandates of separation of church and state.

The case, *Santa Fe Independent School District v. Jane Doe* (99-62), will test federal court decisions that struck down a Galveston County, Texas, school board policy of allowing such prayers as a violation of church and state.

The high court's ruling, expected by late June, will be the court's first major school-prayer decision since its 1992 ruling in *Lee v. Weisman* (112 S. Ct. 2649), when it banned clergy-led prayers such as invocations and benedictions at public school graduation ceremonies.

Conflicting Rulings

Legal experts expect the ruling to clarify the muddled case law on the issue. For example, the 11th Circuit Court of Appeals ruled in Atlanta held that school districts are free, if not obliged, to allow student-led prayers.

Four students in 1995 challenged the Santa Fe Independent School District's policy of allowing students to deliver a "message" or "invocation" over the public address system at home football games and to lead prayers at graduation ceremonies.

The high court's review will be limited to prayers at football games.

A federal judge had ruled that the district's policy of allowing student-led prayers at football games and graduations is allowed only if the prayers are "nonsectarian and non-proselytizing." But ultimately a three-judge panel of the 5th Circuit Court of Appeals voted 2-1 to strike down the policy, holding that football games are "hardly the sober type of annual event that can be appropriately solemnized with prayer."

When the full 5th Circuit refused to rehear the school district's case, officials appealed to the high court.

The school district's attorneys argued in briefs to the Supreme Court that the policy best honors the Constitution's position on religion because it encourages "the neutral accommodation of student viewpoints, whether they be sectarian, ecumenical or religion-free...." It would worse constitutionally if the policy allowed "government censorship of the content of student prayers," the attorneys said.

Eight other states—Alabama, Colorado, Kansas, Louisiana, Mississippi, Nebraska, South Carolina and Tennessee–wrote supporting court briefs in favor of the policy. But the families who succeeded in lower circuits in overturning the policy said it makes people who are of minority religions feel excluded.

"The fact that graduation prayers or prayers before football games are led by students does not diminish the pressure to religious conformity," they wrote. "If anything, it may increase it."

People For The American Way (PFAW) is preparing a friend-of-the-court brief in support of the families' position.

"People who attend school football games are a captive audience for what is presented on the public address system," said Elliot Mincberg, legal director for PFAW. "A person's choice about whether to participate in a prayer, or the type of prayer he may wish to participate in, is taken away when an invocation is broadcast to the entire audience."

Court Rules Student-Led Prayers Legal in Alabama

A federal appeals court July 14, 1999, reversed a judge's ruling barring students from praying or leading prayers in Alabama schools.

In a unanimous decision of a three-judge panel, the 11th U.S. Circuit Court of Appeals in Atlanta ruled that a lower court was wrong to restrict student-initiated prayers at DeKalb County schools.

The appeals court in *Chandler v. DeKalb County Public Schools* (97-6898) deemed "the suppression of student-initiated religious speech" neither necessary nor helpful in achieving "constitutional neutrality towards religion." But the appeals court did not reject the lower court's restrictions that school officials may not lead prayers or other religious activities.

The American Civil Liberties Union lauded the court's action. "School teachers still can't grab students and ask them to pray in class," said Pamela Sumners, an attorney for the group.

Michael Chandler, the former vice principal of Valley Head High School, sued the district in 1997, claiming it illegally promoted Christianity at athletic events, distributed Bibles and allowed teacher-led devotionals.

Court Bans Student-Led Prayers at Graduation

A federal appeals court has temporarily barred a Florida school district from allowing seniors to vote on whether to have prayers at graduation ceremonies, saying the practice violates the Constitution.

"The Duval County school system developed this policy as an attempt to circumvent [the law] and continue the practice of prayer, and to permit sectarian and proselytizing prayer, at graduation ceremonies," wrote Chief Judge Joseph Hatchet of the 11th Circuit Court of Appeals for the majority.

"The Duval County school system exerted tremendous control over the graduation ceremonies," as it should, but allowing students to decide by majority vote whether to have religious exercises at graduation "creates a danger that a majority will bring intimidating pressures to bear in favor of a particular religion," said Hatchet in delivering the 2-1 decision in *Adler et al. v. Duval County School Board* (98-2709) in May 1999.

Vote for Prayers

After two major court decisions in 1992 that barred school-sponsored prayer at graduations, Duval officials issued guidance to schools on how to allow students to lead prayer at graduation ceremonies without violating the Constitution's prohibition against state involvement in religion.

Duval officials sought to change a previous policy of no prayers at graduation ceremonies by relying on the 5th Circuit Court of Appeals decision in *Jones v. Clear Creek Independent School District* (9977 F.2d 963) and the U.S. Supreme Court's ruling in 1992 *Lee v. Weisman* (505 U.S. 577).

The 1992 *Jones* decision upheld a Texas school district's policy allowing "nonproselytizing prayers" at graduation ceremonies. The Supreme Court twice refused to review that decision, letting it stand as law in Texas, Louisiana and Mississippi. But in the same year, the high court in *Lee* banned prayers at graduation ceremonies that are directed and initiated by the school system.

Based on those rulings, Duval school officials allowed individual schools to offer students a vote on whether to have prayers at graduation ceremonies and to permit the opening and closing message to be delivered by a student volunteer, chosen by the senior class as a whole. The content of the message was solely up to the student.

Former Students Sue

In 1993, former students Emily Adler and Seth Finke sued the Duval County public school system, saying the school-issued guidance "constituted an establishment of religion and infringed on their free exercise of religion." Both the federal district and appeals courts denied the students' request to ban the policy, or classify the case a class-action and award them money damages because the students had graduated.

In May 1998, Adler and Finke filed another suit against the district on the same grounds, asking the court to bar the system's prayer policy and require the district to pay money damages.

The district court again ruled in favor of the school system. But this time the students won favor from the appeals court.

"The overriding issue in this case is whether the Duval County school system's policy ... effectively dissociates any prayer that may occur at the graduation ceremonies from state control," Hatchet said.

"An impermissible practice cannot be transformed into a constitutionally acceptable one by putting a democratic process to an improper use," Hatchet said, quoting a 1993 3rd Circuit ruling in *New Jersey v. Black Horse Pike Regional Board of Education* (94-5233). That decision banned a practice allowing senior class leaders to poll their class to gauge support for prayer or a moment of silence at graduation.

Hatchet said Duval's guidance also violated the high court's three-prong test set in *Lemon v. Kurtzman* (403 U.S. 602, 1971), which said a policy is illegal if it does not have a secular purpose, if it promotes religion or if it creates an excessive government entanglement in religion. But Judge Stanley Marcus disagreed, saying the majority misapplied the Supreme Court's Establishment Clause jurisprudence by viewing the student-led prayers as government actions and the student-selected prayer leaders as actors of the state.

"The majority opinion has come perilously close to pronouncing an absolute rule that would excise all private religious expression from a public graduation ceremony, no matter how neutral the process of selecting the speaker may have been, nor how autonomous the speaker was in crafting his message," he said.

Hatchet temporarily banned Duval's policy and sent *Adler v. Duval County School Board* (98-2709) back to the District Court for the Middle District of Florida for further review.

Court Bars Prayers before School Board Meetings

A federal appeals court in Ohio banned a Cleveland school board's policy of opening public meetings with prayer because the practice violates the Constitution.

But the 2-1 decision of the U.S. Sixth Circuit Court of Appeals represents how complicated the issue has become, with split decisions across circuits and the Supreme Court's refusal to take up the issue in recent years.

"We do not mean to imply that religion must be kept entirely out of the public school system," said Judge Ronald Lee Gilman, in delivering the March 1999 majority opinion *in Coles et al. v. Cleveland Board of Education* (97-3082).

"Certainly students might themselves wish to pray during the time they spend at school. It is only when the government, through its school officials, chooses to introduce and exhort religion in the school system that Establishment Clause concerns take shape."

The Establishment Clause prohibits government-sponsored religion. Gilman said the Cleveland board's involvement in promoting prayer "crossed the line of constitutional infirmity."The board began opening meetings with prayer after the 1992 board elections. Newly elected board president Lawrence Lumpkin announced then that the new seven-member board would begin all board meetings with prayers, which usually included references to Jesus and were said by Christian members of the community selected by Lumpkin.

With conflicting opinions from two lower courts well-supported by opposing precedents, Gilman said this case does not "neatly fit" into the Supreme Court's prohibitions against school-sponsored prayer set in *Lee v. Weisman* 9505 U.S. 577 (1992). The high court in that case ruled that opening prayers at graduation ceremonies violate the Establishment Clause of the First Amendment.

But, Gilman said, it also does not fall into the same category as the public prayers allowed in the high court's *Marsh v. Chambers* 463 U.S. 783 (1983) ruling, permitting opening prayers at legislative sessions.

The majority based its decision on the Supreme Court's 1971 *Lemon v. Kurtzman* (403 U.S. 602) ruling, which said a state-sponsored activity will not violate the Constitution if it has a secular purpose, does not advance or inhibit religion, or does not create an excessive entanglement of government with religion. Failing on any of those conditions constitutes a violation of law, legal experts say.

The Sixth Circuit held that the Cleveland school board failed all three tests because the motivations of the officials were unclear and prayers were not necessary to connote solemnity at the meetings.

Also, the court said the board's prayers did not meet the sectarian requirements of the law because they were consistently Christian and the board president's involvement in promoting and arranging the prayers created an excessive entanglement.

But Judge James Ryan disagreed, arguing that the majority misapplied the *Lemon* test, and that the school board's opening prayer falls under the Supreme Court's *Marsh* ruling allowing prayers at legislative sessions. "In *Marsh*, the case most analogous to this case, the Supreme Court acknowledged the existence of the *Lemon* test, but did not apply it," he wrote.

"Far be it for me to run ahead of the United States Supreme Court. If that Court is satisfied that the *Lemon* factors did not apply to prayer before a legislative or 'other deliberative body,' I am satisfied they do not apply to the deliberations of the Cleveland Board of Education," Ryan wrote.

The majority sided with former John Adams High School student Sarah Coles and high school math teacher Gene Tracy, who sued the district jointly in 1992 after they publicly objected to the board's opening prayers and were rebuffed.

But nationally, the issue continues to build steam with conflicting court rulings and appeals that experts say may force a Supreme Court review. For example, a Texas school board will appeal a Fifth Circuit Appeals Court decision that bars school-sponsored prayers before football games.

RELIGIOUS GROUPS, TEXTS

U.S. Court Bans Discrimination Against School Religious Groups

A federal district court ruled in January that an Oregon school system may not bar religious clubs from meeting on school property because of their religious identity.

Judge Michael R. Hogan of the U.S. District Court for the District of Oregon issued a permanent ban against an Oakridge School District policy that banned religious groups from meeting in elementary schools and prohibited students and faculty from handing out religious materials. Non-religious groups were allowed to meet and distribute materials.

The ruling in *Culbertson v. Oakridge School District* (96-6216) ordered the school district to offer religious groups the same access and privileges offered to secular groups.

Schools Have Legal Right To Bar Bible Stories

A New Jersey school district did not violate the rights of a first-grade student by preventing him from reading a Bible story in class, a federal appeals court ruled last October.

The student and his mother, identified in court records only as Z.H. and C.H., respectively, sued the Medford Township Board of Education, alleging that school officials violated the boy's First Amendment rights by barring him from reading the story of Jacob to his first-grade class.

The family also claims school officials violated Z.H.'s freedom of speech rights in the previous school year, when he was in kindergarten, by not displaying Z.H.'s poster of Jesus, which he submitted after students were asked to draw something for which they are thankful.

Pointing to U.S. Supreme Court precedents, two courts—the U.S. District Court for the District of New Jersey and now the appeals court—disagreed that school officials acted illegally.

"We conclude that plaintiff has failed to allege a violation of Z.H.'s First Amendment right to freedom of expression because the defendants' restrictions on Z.H.'s speech were reasonably related to legitimate pedagogical concern," wrote Judge Walter Stapleton of the 3rd Circuit Court of Appeals in the Oct. 22 ruling in *C.H. et al. v. Oliva et al.* (98-5061).

Stapleton referred to legal theories established in a number of related U.S. Supreme Court decisions, including the 1988 *Hazelwood School District v. Kuhlmeier* (484 U.S. 260), which gave school officials the right to control "the style and content" of student speech in school-sponsored activities "so long as their actions [to limit speech] are reasonably related to legitimate pedagogical concerns."

In addition to barring speech that advocates reckless or illegal behavior in school publications and productions, the law gives officials the right to curb expression on everything from the existence of Santa Claus in elementary schools to teenage sexual activity for older students. The facts in the current case fell within the legal realm of school prerogative.

First-grade teacher Grace Oliva of Haines Elementary School in Medford, N.J., gave her students an assignment to bring in their favorite book from home and read one of the stories to class. She then reviewed the books before they were read to the students.

Z.H. brought in "The Beginner's Bible: Timeless Children's Stories" to read the story of Jacob and his 12 sons from Genesis. Oliva, whose decision was supported by other school officials contacted about the matter, told Z.H. that he could not read the story because it might offend students from other religions in the class.

Instead, Oliva told him he could read it to her when the other students were not in class.

The year before, Z.H.'s kindergarten teacher had asked students to draw pictures of what they are thankful for. Although Z.H.'s picture of Jesus was posted with those drawn by other students, school officials later took it down.

Schools Can't Use Clergy in Classrooms, Court Says

A program at a Texas school district that brings clergy to schools to serve as counselors to students is unconstitutional, a federal appeals court ruled last spring.

The U.S. 5th Circuit Court of Appeals overturned a lower court ruling in favor of the Beaumont Independent School District's "Clergy in the Schools" program.

The lower court, which rendered its ruling in favor of the district before the case went to trial, held that the students, identified only as "the Does" in court records, failed to identify a personal injury suffered due to this program. Students are free to decline to participate in the program.

But the appeals court disagreed.

"The Does have alleged sufficient injury—more precisely, sufficient threatened injury—to establish their standing to challenge the program," wrote Judge Jacques Wiener for the 2-1 majority decision in *Doe v. Beaumont Independent School District* (97-40429).

"The Doe children attend schools in which the program operates, and they are continually at risk of being selected [for the program] by [the district's] administrators, without advance notice and without parental consent."

Clergy in Class

The Beaumont program brings local clergy into schools twice a year and selects student participants of various races, religions and socio-economic classes. Protestant Christian clergy are mostly invited, school officials say, because of their prominence in the local community.

The clergy are told not to pray with children, and they are also barred from discussing sex and abortion. School officials direct clergy to limit discussion topics to civic duties, but they also may discuss items related to divorce.

The appeals court said the Beaumont program fails all three tests set by the Supreme Court's decision in the 1971 *Lemon v. Kurtzman* case (403 U.S. 602), which set the standard by which religious activities in the public domain are judged to determine whether they violate the constitutional prohibition of government involvement in religion.

The high court's *Lemon* decision said a state-sponsored activity will not violate the Constitution if it has a secular purpose, does not advance or inhibit religion, or does not create an excessive entanglement of government with religion. Failing on any of those conditions constitutes a violation of law, according to legal experts.

A 'Damoclean' Threat

That the Does are compelled by law to attend schools in which the program is ongoing creates a level of "Damoclean threat [that] removes the Does' claim from the realm of generalized grievance and provides the degree of 'concrete adverseness' necessary for the adjudication of constitutional issues," Weiner said.

Further, "the chances of one of the Doe children being selected are real, not merely the extremely remote odds of a lightning strike or lottery win," he said. "This is precisely the kind of threat of personal and direct non-economic injury that is actionable under the Establishment Clause."

The majority opinion directed the U.S. District Court for the Eastern District of Texas to review the case and issue orders to block the program, render judgment consistent with the appeals court opinion and award the families attorneys' fees and costs.

Judge Emilio Garza was the lone dissenter on the three-judge panel.

He argued the program did not operate in a manner that would violate the Establishment Clause because of the voluntary nature of the program and students' ability to decline participation. He also noted that school administrators are required to attend the clergy-led meetings to ensure there is no violation of church-state law.

South Carolina Religion Classes Don't Break Law

A school system policy that allows students to travel off campus to study religion is legal, an attorney told school officials from South Carolina.

Former U.S. Justice Department attorney Bruce Davis told Clover, S.C., school board members and administrators that they do not violate the First Amendment by allowing student to meet once a week at local churches and in a mobile classroom.

"There has been a lot of what I consider blatant misinterpretation of the law," he told the board in September.

"The basic principle of a public entity … is to be neutral in matters of religion." Davis spoke to officials at the request of the district's Bible Studies Released Time Committee, a group that sponsors off-campus religious studies in Clover.

Under pressure from city residents, the school board in 1997 ended the practice of allowing voluntary, on-campus religious studies. The current program is funded entirely by local churches, so no state supervision is necessary.

Supreme Court Precedent

Davis—who, in addition to working for Justice, also served as a private attorney for schools and as an assistant to the South Carolina attorney general—pointed to a 1952 Supreme Court case that approved off-campus religious studies for students.

The high court ruled in *Zorach v. Clausen* (343 U.S 306) that students may partake in off-campus religious studies during school hours as long as the program does not take place at a school facility and the religious group fully funds and operates the course.

In fact, Davis pointed out the Supreme Court in that case ruled that not allowing students time to study religion would violate the First Amendment because it would be a statement against religious freedom.

Robert Boston, a spokesman for Americans United for Separation of Church and State, said the circumstance is the one issue within the realm of religion in schools that is clearly sanctioned by the Supreme Court. "But school districts across the country usually don't opt to offer off-campus religious studies because the school day is already so short," he said.

Davis did warn the South Carolina school district that it could be in danger of violating the law if the religious course is held in its mobile classroom because that could give the impression the district sponsors religious studies. Instead, he told school officials to hold all religious classes at local churches.

South Carlina school officials say 21 school districts offer "released-time" classes, usually for fourth- through sixth-graders.

ACLU Sues over Religious Texts in California

The American Civil Liberties Union has sued a California one school district over the use of textbooks with a religious bent.

The ACLU on Aug. 24, 1999, sued the Belridge School District, near Bakersfield, Calif., for using textbooks that convey specific religious perspectives, including verbatim biblical passages and prayers for students to read.

The suit lists examples from the books, including an introduction to a third-grade American history textbook that reads: "Throughout the history of America, God has heard the prayers of those who love him and their country. The names of many of these praying Christians are not written in history books, but their prayers were heard by God."

The textbook is one of many produced by the religious publisher Beka Book, Inc., used widely in the district for kindergarten through eighth grade students.

The ACLU of Southern California argues in its complaint that the district's use of the textbook violates constitutional prohibitions against publicly funded institutions becoming involved in religious matters and advances Christianity over other religions.

"This is a case about a public school that inculcates students with its own proscribed version of what God is, who God chooses to listen to, and how one gets on God's good side," said ACLU attorney Peter Eliasberg.

"It is shocking that public school officials would trample on religious freedom that way and turn a blind eye to four decades worth of fundamental constitutional principals that flatly forbid public schools from converting classrooms into pulpits in which school officials conduct what amounts to religious exercises and rituals," Eliasberg added.

The lead plaintiffs in the suit are Veronica Van Ry and her 12-year-old daughter, Rita Elliot.

ACLU Sues Chicago District over Boy Scout Affiliation

Schools should not support the Boy Scouts of America as long as scouts are required to take a religious oath, the American Civil Liberties Union is charging in a federal lawsuit.

ACLU's Chicago affiliate, in a lawsuit filed in April 1999, says public funding of the Boy Scouts program violates the separation of church and state. "Government agencies simply cannot spend tax dollars on programs that exclude people because of their religious beliefs," said ACLU attorney Roger Leishman.

The Boy Scout oath begins, "On my honor, I will do my duty for God and my country ..." One of the defendants in the lawsuit, filed on behalf of five taxpayers, is the Chicago public school system. "There is not a single allegation of a particular instance of discrimination on the basis of religion," said Robert Hall, first assistant attorney with Chicago public schools. Instead, the lawsuit, he said, is "based on the philosophy of the Boy Scouts with no particular instance of discrimination alleged, and that's a problem from our standpoint."

Another legal problem, Hall said, is that Chicago is being asked to represent all local government entities in the state. "Due process would require each local government entity to answer the charges on their own behalf," he said.

Hall did not know how many students in Chicago's schools are involved in the scouting organization, but said that figure would be acquired before the district gives its official legal response to the lawsuit within the next month. Gregg Shields, spokesman for the national Boy Scouts of America, called the lawsuit "regrettable."

The city of Chicago broke off its affiliation with the Boys Scouts of America last year following another ACLU lawsuit, which involved both the religious issue as well as the group's ban of gay members. But the city's school district was not involved in that lawsuit and therefore continued its ties with the organization.

Indiana School Board Crafts Its Own 'Commandments'

Instead of contending with the legal problems inherent in posting the Ten Commandments in their schools, a southern Indiana school district is crafting its own version of the rules.

Scottsburg, Ind., school officials say they know posting the Ten Commandments would violate the First Amendment—but what about the 11 "Common Precepts"?

They start with "Trust In God," taken from "In God We Trust," printed on U.S. currency, school officials say. School Superintendent Robert Hooker said in December that stronger morals should be taught in school, given the growing tendency of school violence. "We're just trying to put forth a positive message."

The American Civil Liberties Union (ACLU) is threatening to sue the

Scott County School District if it continues with its plan to post the "behavior code."

"The edict to trust in God is clearly a religious notion," said the ACLU's Kenneth Falk.

North Carolina Schools Want Scripture in Hallways

Alexander County school officials plan to ask the U.S. Supreme Court whether they can post the Ten Commandments in schools because of their historical significance.

County commissioners opted to forgo asking their state lawmakers to allow the Ten Commandments in schools, and instead voted in November 1999 to head straight to the high court.

Two commissioners, Joel Harbinson and John Watts, held that their request would be prohibited under the Constitution's Establishment Clause.

The high court in 1980 barred the posting of the Ten Commandments in schools.

But as an alternative, Harbinson wants schools to post a paraphrase of Jesus' "greatest commandment": "Love God and love one another."

The commissioners are hoping that will skirt the high court's 1980 ruling.

New York Court Bans Religious School District

New York's highest court has ruled illegal a state law that creates a separate school district for the disabled children of a Jewish sect.

This is the third version of the law—which the state legislature has tweaked several times in attempts to create a lawful district for the disabled students in a Hasidic Jewish community—that has been struck down by New York courts and the U.S. Supreme Court.

"The legislation has the impermissible effect of advancing one religious sect" and that is unconstitutional, wrote Court of Appeals of New York

Judge George Smith for the majority in the 4-3 decision in May 1999 in *Grumet v. George Pataki.*

Smith said the law afforded the community an "impermissible accommodation of religion." The U.S. Supreme Court used similar language when it ruled against an earlier version of the law in the 1997 case *Agostini v. Felton* (65 USLW 2524).

Leaders and parents in the Hasidic Jewish community say their disabled children don't learn well in non-Hasidic schools and that their children are traumatized by encountering people outside their culture. But the New York School Board Association, which has successfully fought the bill numerous times, says disabled children can be taught in neighboring school districts.

The majority opinion of the state court said the law fails to keep the government neutral because the creation of a separate school district could be seen as government endorsement of the Hasidic community. This violates the second tenet of a legal test, set by the U.S. Supreme Court, used to determine the legality of government involvement in religious activity.

The high court's 1971 ruling in *Lemon v. Kurtzman* (403 U.S. 602) says a law or government practice is illegal if it does not have a secular purpose; if it primarily promotes religion; or if it creates an excessive government entanglement with religion. Failing any part of the test will render a law or practice illegal.

Judge Joseph Bellacosa wrote for the dissent: "The simple, but well-founded, presumption that an act of the legislature is constitutional ... can be upset only by proof persuasive beyond a reasonable doubt ...

"When the two prior versions of statutory authorization were declared constitutionally faulty, the legislature corrected the identified problems. It is now three times that different legislatures have passed, and different governors have approved, legislation to address the conceded concerns of these needy children with the environment of their civic community."

He said the issue presents a conflict between the constitutional prohibition against government involvement in religion and constitutionally protected rights of association. The U.S. Supreme Court may have to settle the matter once and for all, Bellacosa said.

EVOLUTION

Court Halts Louisiana District's Evolution 'Disclaimer'

Saying that the practice violates the U.S. Constitution, a federal appeals court in Louisiana barred a school district from requiring that all teachers read their classes a disclaimer before introducing evolution theory.

Fifth Circuit Court of Appeals Judge Fortunato Benavides spoke for a three-judge panel in September when he called the district-wide disclaimer mandated by the Tangipahoa Parish Public Schools a "sham" and a violation of the First Amendment's prohibition against government establishment of religion.

The disclaimer, passed by a 5-4 board vote on April 19, 1994, generally states that the scientific theory of evolution "should be presented to inform students of the scientific concept and not intended to influence or dissuade the Biblical version of creation or any other concept."

It also offers students a "recognition" by the board that "it is the basic right and privilege of each student to form his/her own opinion and maintain beliefs taught by parents on this very important matter of the origin of life and matter."

It goes on to encourage students to "exercise critical thinking" and "closely examine each alternative toward forming an opinion." But two courts found that the board's disclaimer did not aim to encourage "critical thinking." Instead, they said, it does just the opposite.

"We find that the disclaimer as a whole furthers a contrary purpose, namely the protection and maintenance of a particular religious viewpoint," wrote Benavides in the Aug. 13 ruling of *Freiler v. Tangipahoa Parish School Board* (97-30879; 98-30132).

"From this, schoolchildren hear that evolution as taught in the classroom need not affect what they already know," he said. "Such a message is contrary to an intent to encourage critical thinking, which requires that students approach new concepts with an open mind and a willingness to alter and shift existing viewpoints."

The disclaimer fails legal tests set by several Supreme Court precedents, Benavides wrote. As an example, in *Agostini v. Felton* (521 U.S. 203, 117 S.Ct. 1997), the high court ruled that a state program or action fails its three-prong test when it fails to have a secular purpose, establishes a preference for one religion or fosters excessive government entanglement with religion. Failing any one of the tests results in a constitutional violation.

"The disclaimer, taken as a whole, encourages students to read and meditate upon religion in general and the 'Biblical version of Creation' in particular," Benavides said.

"Although it is not, per se, unconstitutional to introduce religion or religious concepts during school hours, there is a fundamental difference between introducing religion and religious concepts in an appropriate study of history [or other subjects], and reading a School Board-mandated disclaimer," he wrote.

The issue surfaced in Kansas in August, where a school board voted to teach creation science instead of evolution. Legal experts predict lawsuits.

ACLU Warns of Lawsuits Following Evolution Vote

After Kansas state education board banished the topic of evolution from state standards and assessments last summer, civil libertarians have put educators there on notice not to teach elements of so-called "creation science."

The American Civil Liberties Union (ACLU) sent letters to Kansas school districts warning of potential lawsuits should schools teach creationism in the absence of evolution theory in biology classrooms.

"The law in this area is clear," the ACLU letter said. "States and school districts may not adopt religious theories as standards in school curricula, nor may they restructure their curricula for the purpose of omitting accepted scientific theories which may conflict with particular religious beliefs." The state board's 6-4 decision last August essentially lets local school boards decide what tenets of evolution or creationism to include in instruction.

Several other states, including Ohio and Tennessee, have sought to include creationism in science instruction, but those efforts have been struck down repeatedly by the U.S. Supreme Court.

"Having failed to succeed at forcing ... creation-science on public school students, proponents of creationism are now resorting to the tactic of removing essential scientific instruction," said Jay Barrish, president of the ACLU's affiliate board.

"We think the courts will ultimately see this tactic for what it is—a blatantly unconstitutional attempt to introduce a specific religious viewpoint into the classroom," he added.

While cheered by religious conservatives, the incident has brought worldwide ridicule upon Kansas and threatened the state's image. "This is a terrible, tragic, embarrassing solution to a problem that didn't exist," Gov. Bill Graves, a Republican, said after the decision.

He later expressed hopes that the incident would spur legislators to strip the board of its power through constitutional amendment and replace it with an appointed education secretary. But state board members pledged to fend off attempts to reduce their role in setting education policy.

While many urban districts in Kansas say they don't plan ending instruction on evolution, proponents of creation science are already trying to get the concept taught in at least one Kansas district.

Parents in the Pratt school district, a small prairie town about 60 miles west of Wichita, want their local school board to adopt the book "Of Pandas and People," which stresses the concept of "intelligent design" over evolution. But critics say since intelligent design is a euphemism for creation science, the book doesn't pass muster for use in schools.

GAY/SPECIAL INTEREST GROUPS

Court To Eye Utah District's 'Ban' on Gay Youth Group

A federal appeals court will decide whether a Utah school district's policy of allowing only curriculum-related groups to meet after school discriminates against a gay student alliance.

A lower court has already ruled that the updated policy of the Salt Lake City school district does not violate the First Amendment, sparking the students to appeal to the 10th Circuit Court of Appeals.

"The [policy] remains neutral on matters of viewpoint so long as the subject matter of a student group may be shown to be directly related to the curriculum," wrote Judge Bruce Jenkins of the U.S. District Court of Utah in January in declaring the policy legal.

But his ruling isn't as simple as that. Jenkins also said the school district violated the rights of students of the East High Gay/Straight Alliance during the 1997-98 school year, when school policy at the time created what legally is considered a "limited public forum."

The U.S. Supreme Court has held that such a forum is created when a public entity, such as a school, makes its property generally available to a class of speakers, Jenkins held.

During that time, the students argue in the lawsuit, the school had allowed a variety of groups to meet on campus, such as the Future Homemakers of America, and not all of them were related to the school's curriculum. The gay students accuse the school of refusing them access to school facilities on the basis of objecting to their views on homosexuality.

"Where a state university or public school makes its facilities generally available for the activities of student groups, it has designated those facilities as a 'limited public forum' and generally cannot discriminate among those groups because of their content or subject matter," Jenkins continued, referring to the students' rights of speech and association.

School Corrects Problem

When the school system amended its 1996 policy to create a closed fo-rum—allowing only those groups with curriculum-related purposes to meet on campus—it corrected its previous violation of the Equal Access Act of 1990.

Congress passed the act to bar the denial of "noncurricular student groups' meetings on the basis of subject matter, namely religious, politi-cal, philosophical or other content of speech."

Both the school and the gay students unsuccessfully sought pretrial judgments on whether the school's policy constitutes an illegal, unwrit-ten ban at the school on "gay-positive views."

Jenkins ultimately ruled in a pretrial hearing that the school's amended policy does not violate federal law currently, but he also ruled that the policy in place during 1997-98 did violate the students' speech and ac-cess rights.

The students—who are seeking nominal damages and the right to meet on campus—are appealing the portion of Jenkins' ruling that favors the school district's current policy of banning their group because it is not considered to be tied to the school curriculum.

Authority Questioned

A series of Supreme Court decisions guides school authorities in setting limits for groups meetings on campus.

While the high court's 1969 *Tinker v. Des Moines Independent School Dis-trict* (393 U.S. 503, 89 S. Ct. 733, 21 L.Ed. 2d 731) affirms students' First Amendment rights to "engage in non-disruptive expression on school premises," a later case clarifies a school board's authority in such matters.

Bethel School District v. Fraser (478 U.S. 675, 106 S. Ct. 3159, 92 L.Ed. 2d 549) held that the "determination of what manner of speech in the classroom or in school assembly is inappropriate properly rests with the school board."

The Salt Lake City school district invoked these and other cases to jus-tify its action barring the students' from meeting during the 1997-98 school year.

But Jenkins said that the district's "analysis blurs the distinction between the power and discretion of school officials to select appropriate subject matter and materials to be taught in the school's curriculum, and the relatively limited power of school officials to restrict or proscribe student expression of student views."

Schools do not have "broad discretion to regulate student expression in the context of student clubs and groups meeting on school premises during non-instructional time, or to discriminate against or exclude a particular student viewpoint from an existing forum," he ruled in *East High Gay/Straight Alliance v Board of Education* (00-4003).

The 10th Circuit has not yet acted on the appeal. A similar lawsuit filed by California students ended with a federal judge overturning a school board's refusal to let a gay-straight club meet on school grounds.

California School Must Let Gay Rights Group Meet on Campus

A gay tolerance club made up of students attending a California high school is allowed to meet, pending litigation to determine whether a school district may bar them from gathering.

The U.S. District Court for the Central District of California on Feb. 4, 2000, gave El Modena High School students a preliminary victory by granting their request for interim permission to meet.

The students accuse Orange County Unified School District officials of violating their free speech rights by forbidding them to meet after school, while allowing other extracurricular groups to meet. Judge David Carter granted the students request because without "the threat of a litigation and court-ordered enforcement of the students' rights, [school officials] were unlikely ever to recognize the club."

Citing high rates of suicide among gay teens, the judge also said the students have been "injured not only by the board's excessive delay, but also by the inability to effectively address the hardships they encounter at school every day."

School officials are appealing the order, but Carter refused to stay his ruling pending the appeal. They say in court papers that they rejected the club because it covers issues already discussed in the human sexuality curriculum.

But students Anthony Colin, 15, and Heather Zetin, 16, said their Gay-Straight Alliance Club is intended as a forum to address discrimination. The school allows clubs for Christians and ethnic minorities.

Boy Scouts Case Not Likely To Alter School Policy

Despite the close relationship the Boy Scouts of America maintains with public schools around the country, a case set to go before the Supreme Court that examines the group's right to bar homosexuals, among others, isn't likely to affect schools at all.

The high court agreed without comment Jan. 14, 2000, to consider the issues raised by *Boy Scouts of America v. Dale* (99-699).

The case presents the question of whether the Boy Scouts, as a private organization, has a constitutional right to ban members on the basis of sexual orientation. It involves James Dale, an assistant scoutmaster, who was expelled because scout officials learned he is gay.

In that case, the New Jersey Supreme Court last year ruled that organized Scouting is a public institution that is barred by law from discrimination, rejecting the Scouts' argument that it is a private organization.

The New Jersey court ruled against the Scouts, arguing in part that the group has a close relationship with public schools, which sponsor some troops and offer recruitment opportunities through their enrollments.

But Julie Underwood, general counsel at the National School Boards Association, said public schools' relationship with the Scouts is similar to its association with other groups.

"We allow churches and all sorts of other groups to meet at schools," she said. The use of a school as a community rental facility or by a student club is ruled by the Equal Access Act, whose principles were affirmed in the 1986 Supreme Court case *Bender v. Williamsport* (106 S. Ct. 1326).

The high court's ultimate decision in *Bender* addressed a technicality pertaining to the appeal, but the lower court's ruling remained intact and unchallenged, holding that school districts may not bar groups from meeting on campus based on their religious affiliations or requirements.

Underwood pointed out that school districts, under First Amendment legal standards, are not required to permit disruptive, obscene, harmful or pervasively vulgar groups on their campuses. "Otherwise, we do not get involved in groups' membership requirements," she said.

'To God and My Country'?

An unrelated case in Chicago involves a challenge to the Scouts' requirement that its members affirm a belief in God. Scout programs in the Windy City are operated by local schools, which the American Civil Liberties Union says violates the Constitution's Equal Protection and Establishment clauses.

That case, *Winkler et al. v. Chicago School Reform Board of Trustees* (99-2424), challenges the degree to which government institutions may be involved with private organizations whose policies are illegal in the public realm.

Last month, the U.S. District Court for the Northern District of Illinois rejected the school district's argument that the American Civil Liberties Union failed to state a legally valid claim. A trial has not yet been scheduled. The Supreme Court is hoping to hear arguments in the *Dale* case this spring and issue a ruling by July.

"When schools are responsible for a program, picking its members and volunteers, our belief is that it violates the [Constitution] to require religious oaths, or to have a program off-limits to people who don't share those beliefs," said Roger Leishman, senior staff attorney for the Illinois ACLU. About 10 percent of Scout troops are sponsored by public schools nationally, he said.

STUDENT EXPRESSION

Kansas Boy's Suspension in Confederate Flag Case Sticks

A federal district court in Kansas upheld the suspension of a boy who violated school policy by drawing a Confederate flag in class.

The boy claimed that Derby Middle School officials violated his First Amendment rights when they suspended him for drawing the flag. But Derby school officials said the boy knew he was violating the school district's strict policy against possessing any symbols of racial intimidation in school.

And the court agreed.

The boy, whose full name does not appear in court records because he is a minor, "drew the flag with an intention of displaying it to another student, and he did so," said Judge Wesley Brown, of the United States District Court for the District of Kansas.

"To put it charitably, the court finds that [he] demonstrated a 'convenient memory' when he recounted those events," Brown said in *West v. Derby Unified School District* (98-1163).

"It is clear to the court that he knowingly and intentionally violated policy against possession of such symbols in school," he said.

The policy, modeled after the district's smoking and sexual harassment policies, was crafted in 1995 after a number of clashes between white and black students heightened racial tensions.

The student, who is appealing the ruling, claimed he was unaware of the policy and that his First Amendment rights protect him from being punished for drawing the flag.

But several school officials said they reviewed the policy with the boy during a number of previous incidents. The policy also is in the student handbook, which students are required to review and get signed by their parents, according to court records.

Several students said they warned him not to draw the flag, but the boy expressed a lack of concern for violating the policy, the records said.

The court ultimately ruled that the First Amendment guarantees "wide freedom in matters of adult public discourse," but students in public schools do not have the same freedom when the result is class disruption.

Students Need School OK To Hand Out Condoms

Illinois school officials had a legal right to disqualify a former high school student from a student election because he handed out condoms without their permission, a federal appeals court ruled in December.

"It is well within the district's rights to disqualify [the boy] for his actions in distributing material that ran counter to the district's pedagogical concern and its educational mission," wrote Judge Roger Wollman in his ruling in favor of the school.

Adam Henerey won the race for junior class president in April 1997. But St. Charles High School Principal Jerry Cook stripped him of his win because he handed out condoms on the morning of the election, in violation of a School Board rule that students seek approval from the principal or assistant principal before handing out any material.

Henerey, who was a sophomore at the time of his election and now is an 18-year old freshman at the University of Missouri, promptly sued the school for violating his free speech rights.

Wollman pointed to several U.S. Supreme Court decisions to affirm a lower court pre-trial decision rejecting Henerey's claim.

Since the election was a school-public activity that did not fall within the realm of a public forum, school officials' had "great" legal authority over the content of candidates' speech," Wollman said in delivering the 2-1 ruling.

Specifically, Wollman cited the high court's 1988 decision in *Hazelwood School District v. Kuhlmeier* (484 U.S. 260), which established that schools "need not tolerate speech that is inconsistent with its pedagogical mission, even though the government could not suppress that speech outside of the schoolhouse."

School administrators had approved Henerey's election slogan, "Adam Henerey, The Safe Choice," but had not approved him giving out condoms attached to stickers bearing his slogan. He gave out 11 condoms.

"At the very least, school districts have an interest in requiring prior notice from anyone proposing to introduce students to information or materials of an explicit sexual nature," he wrote in *Henerey v. City of Charles School District* (98-3439).

Despite the appeals court's acknowledgement that students retain a "high degree of First Amendment protections," Henerey's attorney, Dayna Deck, told the *St. Louis Dispatch* that the 8th Circuit panel doesn't seem to be concerned with "whether high school students have free-speech rights."

She said that if other students are permitted to give out candy as part of their campaigns without getting the approval of school administrators, Henerey should have been permitted to distribute condoms. He was trying to promote prevention of pregnancy and disease, Deck said.

Judge Charles Wolle, who dissented, said the pretrial ruling in favor of the schools by a federal judge was not an appropriate way to settle this case.

"From the principal's approval of materials like candy and buttons distributed by other candidates and refusal to allow Henerey's materials, a jury could well decide it was the message and not the approval process that cost Henerey his junior class presidency."

CHAPTER 5

Funding

The contentious voucher issue has sparked lawsuits around the country over whether public funds should be used to pay tuition at private and, often, religious schools.

The U.S. Supreme Court last year refused to take two Maine cases—*Bagley v. Raymond School Department* and *Strout v. Albanese*—that would have determined whether school districts may use public funds to pay tuition at secular private schools, while refusing payments to religious private schools. The court turned away a similar case from Vermont as well.

Voucher supporters were hoping to garner a high court nod—and both sides of the issue were seeking to resolve inconsistencies among federal courts across the country. For example, lower court decisions in Maine and Vermont conflict with others from Wisconsin and Arizona that ruled constitutional the use of tax dollars to pay tuition at religious schools and to offer tax credits to parents of children at religious schools, respectively.

At the core of the issue is whether the use of public funds at religious schools violates the Constitution's Establishment Clause barring government involvement in religion.

Within the realm of school choice are charter schools, and they also have sparked lawsuits over issues such as student access.

Charter schools differ from public schools in that they are permitted to operate outside of the usual regulations for public schools in return for improving student achievement.

Carrie Ausbrooks, who heads the University of North Texas' Center for Education Reform, gave school attorneys at a recent legal conference a few tips on how charter schools might stay out of legal hot water.

She pointed to the 1993 Tennessee Supreme Court case, *Tennessee Small School Systems v. McWherter*, in which the court ruled that the state's equal protection clause mandated that charter schools be open to all students.

"All state constitutions also contain equal protection clauses that closely mirror the 14th Amendment," said Ausbrooks, who also is a professor of educational administration. "Lawsuits that would fail under the 14th Amendment may still succeed in state scrutiny employed by some state courts and create more fertile ground for litigation involving charter schools." She also suggested that school administrators ensure that ethnic minorities and low-income students are not underrepresented and that transportation is made available to allow all students access to the school.

Recently, school districts strapped for cash have sued their respective states, alleging that funding formulas designed to even out differences within tax bases disadvantage students in poor school districts.

But those districts have not been successful in federal courts: Numerous school districts in Wisconsin and Pennsylvania failed to convince federal courts that state funding formulas are discriminatory.

Some judges have gone so far as to tell the plaintiff school districts, along with citizens and others who sign on, to stop whining about needing more money. But their rulings are based on the U.S. Supreme Court's 1973 opinion in *San Antonio v. Rodriguez*, which approved Texas' funding formula despite funding disparities among districts.

"Those disadvantaged by public school funding systems continue to turn to state courts seeking a judicial declaration that the existing funding system is unconstitutional," wrote two legal experts in a paper on the subject.

Funding reform advocates litigate the issue hoping to garner a favorable court decision that will spur legislative reform, wrote John Dayton, an education law professor at the University of Georgia.

Gerald Bass, a professor of education finance at the University of North Dakota, co-authored the paper, delivered at a recent Education Law Association conference. But the pair note that advocates for funding equity have achieved some legal success. For example, to date, 17 state supreme courts have ruled funding systems unconstitutional; 18 state high courts have upheld them.

VOUCHERS

Supreme Court Turns Away Two Maine Voucher Cases

The Supreme Court in October allowed Maine to use public funds to pay tuition for children at secular private schools while refusing to offer the same support to children attending religious private schools.

The high court, without comment, turned away two appeals that challenged a Maine statute allowing the state to pay for students without a local public school to attend neighboring public or private secular schools in their area. The voucher program pays the equivalent of the state's tuition costs directly to the schools, but religious schools are excluded.

The court's denial of *Bagley v. Raymond School Department* (99-163) and *Strout v. Albanese* (99-254) sets no national precedent and is not expected to stem the national debate over vouchers. But the denial did disappoint voucher supporters, who were predicting the court would accept the appeals, given conflicting rulings within the state.

Vincent McCarthy of the American Center for Law and Justice, who represents the parents and expected the court to accept *Strout*, has argued that Maine already funds private-school education, so "we are saying that [the state has] an obligation not to discriminate against sectarian schools."

But the ruling in *Strout*—which applies only in the 1st Circuit states of Massachusetts, Maine, Rhode Island and New Hampshire, as well as Puerto Rico—affirms lower court opinions that also barred the use of public funds for vouchers to religious schools.

Many school districts in Maine are in sparsely populated areas that do not have their own schools; instead, they pay tuition to neighboring private or public schools. Students have their choice of schools, with the exception of religious schools.

Three parents in *Strout* challenged the state's 1991 law barring the use of state money to pay tuition at religious schools because it would violate the constitutional mandate of separation of church and state. But the 1st Circuit Court of Appeals ruled against them, saying the "Supreme Court has never permitted broad sponsorship of religious schools."

The ruling in *Bagley*, from Maine's Supreme Judicial Court, also upheld the state ban of aid to religious schools. Five families challenged the policy in that case.

Attorneys supporting the plaintiffs of both cases argued that the funds should be considered indirect aid to religious schools because parents decide where it will be sent.

State attorneys rejected that suggestion, pointing to the 1973 Supreme Court ruling in *Committee for Public Education and Religious Liberty v. Nyquist* (413 U.S. 756), which deemed such subsidies a violation of the Constitution's Establishment Clause.

But the high court's 1997 ruling in *Agostini v. Felton* (65 USLW 4524) held that public school teachers can provide remedial help at religious schools.

The justices in October let stand a case that allowed Arizona to give tax breaks to people who donate scholarship money to religious schools.

Pennsylvania State Court Bars District's School Voucher Plan

A Pennsylvania court has ruled illegal a public school district's plan to give students tuition vouchers for private schools in order to ease classroom overcrowding and tax increases.

"The school district clearly acted outside the scope of its authority in adopting the plan," wrote Commonwealth Court of Pennsylvania Judge Rochelle Friedman for a seven-judge panel in December 1999.

The court said Southeast Delco School District violated the state's 1949 Public School Code—which, among other things, regulates school districts' spending practices—when it passed its "School Choice Enrollment Stabilization Plan" in March 1998.

The plan aimed to provide public tuition funds for any student legally residing within the school district who chose to attend any other public or private school.

Avoiding a Potential Liability

A lower court blocked the program from starting in the 1998-99 school year. It would have offered scholarships of $250 to kindergartners, $500 to elementary and middle school students and $1,000 to high school students.

The district had set aside $1.2 million to cover the scholarships, which would be capped at no greater than the amount of state education per-pupil funds received by the district.

The school board justified its school-choice plan with a resolution that said:

- "Parents have a fundamental right to control the education of their children";

- "School choice plays an essential part in improving the quality of education for all Southeast Delco students"; and

- Increased enrollment at already cramped schools will eventually create a "substantial" tax burden on citizens.

The school board pointed out that financially struggling families were taking their children out of private schools and enrolling them in public schools. The district spends about $6,000 to $7,000 annually for each regular public school student, the board said.

"Students who currently attend non-public schools, totaling 1,890 as of January 1997, represent a potential unfunded liability of twelve million dollars per year, or more, for local and state taxpayers," the resolution stated.

Honor the Code

But before the program could start, taxpayers filed a lawsuit asking a trial court to find that the state code prohibits the use of public funds at private schools or those outside the school district.

The school district argued that the state legislature gave it "implied authority" under the School Code to adopt the plan as a means of providing students with the constitutionally mandated "thorough and efficient system of public education."

But the state appeals court affirmed the trial court's holding in favor of the taxpayers in *Giacomucci et al. v. Southeast Delco School District* (98-3060). Pointing to past state Supreme Court opinions and the state constitution, Friedman said the district's arguments did not support the legality of the plan.

"The school district sedulously points out that it is not arguing that the constitutional responsibility of providing a thorough and efficient system of education permits it to over-ride the school code," Friedman said. Falling short of making that argument, the district had no authority to set up the voucher system, she said.

"We are mindful that judicial interference with a school board's performance of its discretionary duties can only be sustained where it is clearly shown that the school board acted outside the scope of its statutory authority or in bad faith," Friedman said. Since that is the case, she said, "we ... enjoin the school district from implementing or enforcing the plan."

Vermont Supreme Court Strikes Down Vouchers

Both the Vermont and U.S. supreme courts last year ruled that vouchers amount to public subsidies of religious education and are illegal.

The Vermont high court ruled last June in *Chittendon Town School District v. Vermont Dept. of Education* (S0478-96) that vouchers violate the state constitution because they "compel taxpayer support of religious worship." The U.S. Supreme Court, without comment, rejected an appeal last Dec. 13.

The Chittendon school district in Vermont does not have a public high school. In March 1996, it approved tuition vouchers for its students to attend a nearby Catholic high school, where tuition is about $3,000 per student. The money would have been paid to the religious school's general fund.

The June 1999 decision affirmed a lower court ruling that also found the district's use of public dollars to pay tuition at religious schools illegal.

"America's children won an important victory," said Bob Chase, who heads the National Education Association. "Now let's get back to the job of improving public education instead of siphoning off scarce public resources for the benefit of a few." Chase's union partially funded the lawsuit.

Americans United for Separation of Church and State also praised the decision.

"There is not this great momentum in the courts for vouchers as advocates say," said Robert Boston, a spokesman for the group. "It shows that most states do have some laws barring the provision of state funds to sectarian institutions."

Voucher advocates were disappointed with the ruling.

"Our program would only allow tuition dollars to go to schools approved by the U.S. Department of Education," said Jeff Spaulding, chairman of Chittendon's school board. But "as long as a school can provide education with a sound curriculum, it doesn't matter whether it's religious."

Spaulding said the state court's decision disappointed him particularly in light of a 1994 case in which the court ruled that a voucher program did not violate the U.S. Constitution.

Last May the 1st Circuit Court of Appeals ruled that a state provision that bars the use of vouchers at religious schools is constitutional. And the Maine Supreme Court ruled on April 3, 1999, that the program's exemption of religious institutions does not violate the Constitution's Establishment Clause or the equal protection provision of the 14th Amendment.

Also in June 1999, the Ohio Supreme Court ruled that state law does not allow funds for the voucher program to come from the state budget. The money must come from a separate allocation.

Ohio Voucher Students Stayed in School This Year

In a partial victory for voucher supporters, a federal judge delayed a temporary ban that would have immediately ended Ohio's voucher program just one business day before the start of the 1999-2000 school year.

U.S. District Judge Solomon Oliver Jr. ruled last August that some 3,200 students who were already attending private schools under the state's embattled voucher program could continue to attend those schools for the fall semester.

But that leaft almost 600 new students who were offered scholarships in March with no tuition funds. Each scholarship is roughly $2,300.

Just two days before, Oliver had imposed an immediate temporary ban on the program while it faced litigation.

The Ohio Education Association, the American Civil Liberties Union and People for the American Way, among others, are suing the state over the program, claiming that it violates constitutional prohibitions against government establishment of religion.

The program gives students tax-supported scholarships to attend schools, including those offering religious education, outside the public school system.

Oliver issued his Aug. 25, 1999, injunction with a 28-page ruling that Cleveland's four-year-old program violates the First Amendment by using taxpayer funds to finance religious schools. "There is no substantial possibility that the voucher program would pass muster under the U.S. Constitution," he ruled.

But even after the judge amended his original ban, the Institute for Justice, which is representing five families who receive publicly funded scholarships to attend private schoolsin Cleveland, said it will continue to appeal the injunction to the 6th Circuit Court of Appeals.

The institute had argued that the original ban would place into chaos the school plans of thousands of children in Cleveland. While the group called the amended ban a "partial victory," it said students may still face mass confusion if they are forced to leave private schools in mid-year.

Not Giving Up

Voucher supporters and the Ohio attorney general filed emergency appeals to the U.S. 6th Circuit Court of Appeals to get the injunction overturned. They vowed, if necessary, to take the case to the U.S. Supreme Court, which has not ruled on the constitutionality of vouchers.

"This is a potential loss for every student and family in Cleveland," declared Clint Bolick, litigation director of the Institute for Justice, a conservative legal group. "We will not let this decision stand without a fight."

Bolick predicted chaos in transferring voucher students to public schools, but city officials pledged to make the transition as smooth as possible.

"The public schools are used to welcoming all children," said Sandra Feldman, president of the American Federation of Teachers. "They will greet them with open arms."

Voucher opponents cheered the ruling and minimized the disruption caused by the court order.

"This is a victory for everyone who cares about our children and our Constitution," said Carole Shields, president of People for the American Way, a liberal advocacy group. "Public dollars should be put to work in the public schools, where they belong, and Ohio's taxpayers should not be forced to subsidize someone else's religion."

In applauding the ruling, Bob Chase, president of the National Education Association, pointed out recent studies that found little overall improvement in student performance as a result of participation in a school-choice program, despite high parental satisfaction.
"The ultimate test of any education reform should be student achievement," he said.

The lawsuit against Cleveland's program was filed by several school and civil liberties groups, including the American Federation of Teachers, the Ohio Education Association, the American Civil Liberties Union, People for the American Way and Americans United for Separation of Church and State.

Milwaukee Choice Schools Break Law, Groups Say

Private and religious schools participating in Milwaukee's citywide choice program are illegally screening applicants and compelling some children to participate in religious activities, according to a complaint filed with Wisconsin's education department.

Advocates for the city's educational system, however, dismissed the detailed allegations as overheated hokum, noting that parents have not filed charges of their own over choice schools and their admissions or educational practices.

The People for the American Way Foundation (PFAW), a liberal advocacy group based in Washington, D.C., and the Milwaukee chapter of the National Association for the Advancement of Colored People (NAACP), last winter wrote to Wisconsin officials to complain aboutthe work of nine of 88 private schools. "Some schools are violating the state's voucher law," PFAW said in a news release, "by charging illegal fees on voucher students, engaging in improper screening and selection of applicants, and violating students' right to religious freedom by actively discouraging parents from opting their children out of religious activities."

A Housing Investigation

In the spring of 1999, PFAW retained the Milwaukee Fair Housing Council, a city board of investigators responsible for evaluating compliance with civil rights statutes, to investigate Milwaukee's voucher schools.

Judith Schaeffer, PFAW's deputy legal director, explained that her group in February had filed a preliminary complaint with the Wisconsin Department of Public Instruction (DPI), saying that admissions material from participating private schools showed they were not selecting from the pool of eligible children.

"Even on paper, they were not complying with the random selection requirements," Schaeffer said, "which makes you wonder what they do in practice."

To find out, Fair Housing Council investigators posed as parents and called the participating private and religious schools, asking what steps were needed to enroll voucher-eligible children.

Under a state court decision that the U.S. Supreme Court refused to review, Wisconsin law allows low-income parents in Milwaukee to choose either secular or religious schools. However, religious schools that volunteer to participate—receiving vouchers worth about $4,900—must let families opt out of their religious educational programs.

According to PFAW, Blessed Trinity Catholic School required parents to sign a pledge committing the child to daily classroom prayer, religion classes and prayer services, and Oklahoma Avenue Lutheran School officials discouraged parents from applying unless their children would participate in religious activities.

"It's a Christian education," the principal of the Oklahoma Avenue Lutheran School said, according to PFAW documents. "That's what we're about."

The allegations involve eight religious schools and one secular institution. In one case, a Montessori school said it would admit children with "previous Montessori experience," according to PFAW documents. The city's investigators also claim that Marquette University High School (MUHS) violated the law's random selection standard by admitting only children who passed an entrance exam and submitted recommendations from educators and pastors.

Sue Smith, vice president for administration at MUHS, denied the charges. Her school requires all applicants to take a placement test—not an admissions exam, she said.

"It's all kind of comical," Smith added, noting that 13 choice students won a lottery to enroll at MUHS. "Everyone whose name was drawn is coming ... The state is very happy about what we're doing."

TUITION PLANS

Supreme Court Immunizes Tuition Plans from Suits

The U.S. Supreme Court ruled last summer that state prepaid college tuition savings plans cannot be sued for violating patents.

The June 1999 decision puts an end to nearly five years of litigation between the New Jersey-based College Savings Bank (CSB) and Florida's prepaid tuition program.

The decision also will allow almost every state to continue operating prepaid tuition plans free from the threat of litigation. CSB claims that almost every state's plan used its method for managing individual accounts.

In the 5-4 decision, the high court ruled in *Florida Prepaid Postsecondary Expense Board v. College Savings Bank* (98-531) that the 11th Amendment shields states from standing trial for trademark or copyright infringement, reversing the opinion of the Federal Circuit Court of Appeals.

That decision was handed down in a suite of four decisions greatly restricting the purview of courts to require states to enforce federal laws in lawsuits brought by individuals. All told, legal analysts predict the decisions could restrict the rights of individuals to take legal actions against public state universities and colleges for infringement of everything from fair labor standards to disabilities law.

Expressing the majority opinion, Chief Justice William Rehnquist wrote, "A state's infringement of a patent, though interfering with a patent owner's right to exclude others, does not by itself violate the Constitution."

That decision has come as a relief to many states that feared they would have to spend time and money staving off CSB's attorneys should the New Jersey Bank win its fight to make the state of Florida stand trial.

"We were concerned that we might have to get into a defensive posture on any type of litigation that is out there, from a resource perspective," said Diana Cantor, executive director of Virginia's prepaid tuition programs."

In 1995, CSB took the Florida prepaid postsecondary education expense board to court for violating its patent on CollegeSure CD, a formula for insuring that long-term investments can cover the cost of college tuition.

While Florida and most state prepaid tuition plans work through partnerships with schools to essentially buy a future share of tuition, CSB argued that the nuts and bolts of the financing for these packages was covered by their CollegeSure patent. As the contractor for Montana's tuition plan, CSB argued it lost business as a result of Florida's patent infringement.

CSB charged that Florida actually encouraged other states to violate its patent when the former director of the state's prepaid tuition plan was also the chief of the trade association for the state plans.

But the question as to whether Florida's tuition plan actually violated CSB's patent was never settled, because the state contended that states—under the 11th Amendment's sovereign immunity provision—were not required to appear in federal court for such matters.

When the federal circuit court of appeals ruled that Florida would have to stand trial, the state appealed the matter to the Supreme Court.

Siding with Florida, the High Court argued that the Patent Remedy Act—legislation that requires states to stand trial for patent infringement—can only be invoked if the state does not take proper steps to compensate the patent holder for loss of property.

PRIVATE SCHOOL FUNDING

Group Sues Wisconsin over Parochial School Subsidies

Advocates for a strict division between religion and the government are suing Wisconsin over a new state technology initiative they say illegally subsidizes parochial schools.

The initiative is part of a multi-million dollar state effort to provide technology resources to schools by offering low-cost, high-speed Internet access.

But an attorney from the Wisconsin-based Freedom from Religion Foundation said the program is illegal because it would let parochial schools use the technology for religious instruction or other sectarian purposes.

"The U.S. Supreme Court's rulings on these issues aren't exactly the model of clarity and consistency," said Jeffrey Kassel, the foundation's attorney. "But the court has been firm that ...when state aid to parochial schools is permitted ...it is aid to the students—not to the schools—and is not to be used for instructional materials."

Kassel filed suit on Nov.4.

Discount Rates for All

The program, Educational Telecommunications Access, offers rock-bottom rates for high-speed Internet access and links to a range of public and private educational institutions.

Approved schools would pay roughly $100 a month for Internet access and special high-speed technology. But the state would pay for the lion's share of the cost, about $600 a month.

Wisconsin officials say the state is expected to begin paying the subsidies next year. "Our position is that the subsidy to schools does not violate either the First Amendment or the Wisconsin Constitution," said Bruce Olsen, a Wisconsin assistant attorney general.

The First Amendment bars government support of religion or religious activities.

"The program has a clear secular purpose to make the subsidy available to both public and private, nonsectarian and secular schools" Olsen said.

But he added that there are no restrictions—"for all kinds of entangled reasons"—that would prevent a private school from using the Internet for religious instruction.

Steven Green, legal director for the Washington, D.C.-based Americans United for Separation of Church and State, said the case is on the "cutting edge of church and state law."

Green said the U.S. Supreme Court has allowed public agencies to "loan" parochial schools textbooks or other materials that could not be used for religious instruction, and that typically are used in public schools.

"But this is an instance where the law has not caught up with advances in educational technology," Green said.

"The thinking—the fiction—of the rulings is that the courts viewed textbooks and other materials as being loaned to students, and not to schools," he said. "But technology has taken off. It is surprising that this hasn't been challenged before."

The foundation's complaint says 26 private schools and 10 colleges have been approved for the subsidies.

STATE SPENDING FORMULAS

Illinois Reforms School Finances—without Court Order

Most states don't revamp their school funding systems unless they are under court order. But a strong economy and a confluence of political forces has made Illinois an exception to that rule.

Gov. Jim Edgar approved a school funding formula that for the first time in Illinois sets a floor for the amount spent per student—with the state making up the difference for less wealthy districts.

"Every Illinois student will be supported by at least the funding level that has been identified as essential," said Joseph Spagnolo, state education chief.

This so-called "foundation level" will grow from $4,100 per student in 1998 to $4,425 for the 2000-01 school year.

The Wages of Sin

Most of the additional state funds for these increases will come from $174 million in higher telephone taxes. The rest comes from "sin taxes:" $100 million from an increased cigarette tax, $57 million from a new riverboat gambling tax, and $11 million from a larger penalty for failure to pay taxes.

The new system—actually plotted by Edgar in 1997 and approved in 1998—also better targets money to districts with high concentrations of low-income students. The state used to give a set amount per low-income student. Now it will give districts with higher concentrations of low-income pupils more funds per child.

In addition, $1.4 billion from school construction bonds will target poorer areas. In fact, the richest districts aren't allowed to get any of that money. Twenty percent of the money is set aside for Chicago.

Courts in 17 states have declared their school financing systems unconstitutional, said Mary Fulton, a policy analyst at the Education Commission of the States. Most recently, the New Hampshire state supreme court ordered the state legislature to come up with a more equitable funding formula.

But the Illinois state supreme court threw out a school funding case several years ago.

"There was not a monumental buildup like in most states," Fulton said. "Rarely do you see a state making changes without outside pressure."

Politically Expedient

What replaced legal pressure was political pressure, observers and officials agreed.

Gov. Edgar, a Republican, had been pushing to cut property taxes and raise state income taxes to boost school funding, but members of his party in the legislature wouldn't go for it.

He called an unusual special session of the legislature to push through his new plan. "Edgar used a series of less offensive taxes, so that was a little more appealing," Fulton said.

Supreme Court Snubs Pennsylvania School Finance Case

The Supreme Court in December denied Pennsylvania immunity from being sued over allegations that its school-funding system discriminates against minority students.

The state had appealed to the high court, seeking to overturn an appeals court decision that allowed private citizens to sue over the funding formula.

But without comment, the high court let stand a Third Circuit Court of Appeals ruling that reinstated the case. A lower court had ruled in favor of the state and dismissed *Ryan, et al. v. Powell (99-527)*.

A 'More Money' Tactic?

The Philadelphia Board of Education, several citizens groups and parents sued Gov. Tom Ridge last year, saying the state allocates less money to K-12 public schools with predominantly minority student enrollments. They accused the state of violating Title VI of the 1964 Civil Rights Act, which bans discrimination in institutions receiving any federal aid.

The state had argued in its high court appeal that people should be barred from suing recipients of federal school funds for violating federal rules that bar discrimination.

Judge Herbert Hutton of the U.S. District Court for the Eastern District of Pennsylvania last December ruled in the state's favor, dismissing the board's and citizens' complaint as "merely a 'we-need-more-money' allegation of a type that has been held non-actionable."

But on Aug. 25, 1999, the Third Circuit Court of Appeals reinstated the lawsuit, saying that private citizens can sue over what they allege are discriminatory effects of school funding systems. The state then unsuccessfully appealed to the Supreme Court.

Ready for Court

Pointing to past Supreme Court rulings on the issue, Pennsylvania officials maintained that Title VI bars *intentional* discrimination exclusively, and only allows the federal government, but not private citizens, to sue for enforcement of the law.

The state argued that the U.S. Education Department overstepped its bounds when it adopted a rule barring school-funding methods that result in unintentional discriminatory effects. "We're ready to represent the facts to the court and prevail," said Tim Reeves, a spokesman for the governor. "There are no smoke and mirrors. We have a color-blind formula."

Unlike many school districts that rely on local funds, Philadelphia asks the state to fund 60 percent of its budget. State officials have argued that the district may indeed need more money, but that doesn't mean the state's method of doling out funds is flawed.

Reeves noted that the state spends an average of $2,800 per student in majority-minority districts, compared with $1,800 per student in mostly white districts. But city officials and parents dispute those figures in a brief opposing the state's high court appeal.

Between 1992 and 1996, school districts with 50 percent or more white students received an average increase of $776 per pupil, while the increase to schools with more than 75 percent minority enrollment was $149 per pupil, they pointed out.

"Pennsylvania's method of funding public education yields racially different results," the brief states. "These intensifying levels of racial discrimination in funding, and the consequent harm to [the children], arise not only from some inadvertent statistical anomaly, but from [the state's] funding decisions made, over time, with prior knowledge of those racially discriminatory consequences."

Fearing that a precedent allowing such suits would besiege other states with litigation, Alabama, New Jersey, Nevada and Utah wrote a supporting brief asking the court to grant the states' appeal. A trial date has not yet been set.

Wisconsin Court Upholds School Funding Formula; Appeal Pending

A Wisconsin appeals court upheld a state formula designed to even out differences in school districts' tax bases, spurring the state Supreme Court in December to take up the case.

The Madison-based Fourth District Court of Appeals agreed with a lower court that the formula does not put students in poor districts at a disadvantage for educational opportunities.

A coalition of school districts, parents, students and taxpayers sued in 1995, claiming the formula set by the legislature in the same year creates an unconstitutional disparity in children's educational opportunities.

The legislature in 1995-96 more than doubled state K-12 education aid from $1.2 billion to $3.1 billion, but the plaintiffs claim that poorer districts struggle with some of the highest taxes and worst facilities in the state as wealthier districts spend lavishly.

No Link to Test Scores

But the December 1998 ruling in *William Vincent v. Joseph Voight* (97-3174) says the 181 plaintiffs represented by the Association for Equity in Funding failed to show that their deteriorating buildings, outdated books and technology and high student-teacher ratios compared to wealthier districts resulted in lower standardized test scores.

In 1996-97, state aid made up 54.6 percent of Wisconsin school funding, with 38.5 percent coming from local property taxes.

The state's formula was based on available state aid, enrollment, costs, local property value per pupil and a guaranteed level of property value per pupil. The state makes up the difference between local property value and the guaranteed state minimum.

Replay of 1989

The unanimous three-judge panel said the low-income districts also failed to prove that the new funding formula is substantially different from the one the Wisconsin Supreme Court upheld in 1989.

The 101 Wisconsin school districts in December 1999 successfully appealed the case to the state Supreme Court, and no date has been set to hear the appeal.

"Categorical aids are distributed without regard to the impact of disparate tax bases among school districts," say the districts' legal briefs.

"This creates extreme differences among school districts in the availability of ... resources."

State officials counter: "We have what is widely recognized as one of the fairest systems in the country.... and we believe the merit falls in favor of the current system."

School finance suits historically have focused on the equity and adequacy of state funding, but in recent years, according to an analysis from the National Conference of State Legislatures, cases have dealt with questions such as the quality of facilities, special education funding or the differences in aid to some types of school districts.

Unlike past cases, which were filed in state courts, two cases were recently filed in federal court, basing their claims on the landmark Civil Rights Act of 1964.

The New York branch of the American Civil Liberties Union filed suit in federal court, charging that students in schools where ethnic and racial minorities make up at least 80 percent of the enrollment are less likely to receive needed educational services than those from predominantly white schools.

The case is the first challenge of a school funding formula under Title VI of the U.S. Civil Rights Act of 1964, according to the report from state legislatures.

Philadelphia school and city officials appealed a federal court decision that Pennsylvania's school funding formula does not discriminate against students based on race and ethnicity.

"The issues of what constitutes an adequate educational system and how it is defined continue to be the main battleground for deciding constitutional from unconstitutional systems," wrote Terry Whitney, who wrote the report.

"Historically, where the system has been upheld, courts have generally said funding for a minimal basic education system was sufficient," she wrote.

CHAPTER 6

Harassment

The U.S. Supreme Court recently clarified school liability in cases in which students sexually harass their peers or are harassed by their teachers.

The landmark 1999 *Davis v. Monroe County Board of Education* set the legal standard for what triggers school liability in student-to-student sexual harassment cases. That ruling was a final link clarifying a legal standard set in an opinion issued before, *Gebser v. Lago Vista Independent School District*.

The rulings established two general legal standards for liability:

- School officials are liable for sexual harassment if they had knowledge of it and failed to act, thereby demonstrating "deliberate indifference." (*Gebser*).

- *Davis* refined that standard by stipulating that the harassment must be "pervasive, severe and objectively offensive" to trigger liability under Title IX of the 1972 Education Amendments, which bar sex discrimination at public institutions.

Legal experts such as Elizabeth Lugg, a law professor at Illinois State University, suggest that school officials take two precautions to limit liability in such cases.

First, districts should adopt a policy, written by either school board members or, better, the school attorney, explicitly stating that sex discrimination and sexual harassment involving students or school staff will not be tolerated. The policy should include a complaint mechanism for alleged victims.

To reinforce the policy, Lugg said schools should hold assemblies for students and workshops for staff members to educate them on sexual harassment.

Once the rules are in place, "follow them!" wrote Lugg in an article published in the *Illinois State School Law Quarterly*.

"This seems like a very obvious suggestion, but often school districts either don't have the time or don't feel they need to follow through on every complaint; only those that seem 'real' or 'credible,'" she said. "But let the procedure determine credibility."

In the *Gebser* case, Lugg said Lago Vista's failure to set up a policy did not qualify as discrimination. But had a policy been in place and not been followed, the court could have ruled that the district was liable for showing "deliberate indifference."

"Avoid even the appearance of deliberate indifference by taking the time to enact policies and procedures required by law and following those procedures when a complaint is made," Lugg said.

Student advocates and school officials lauded *Davis* for clarifying the *Gebser* standard.

School districts criticized *Gebser* for not defining what kind of behavior would trigger Title IX liability, but they praised *Davis* for answering that question with the standard of "pervasive, severe and objectively offensive."

Student advocates applauded *Davis* for holding school districts that deliberately ignore or fail to adequately address such behavior liable under Title IX, as was found to be the case with the Georgia school district named in *Davis*.

STUDENT-TO-STUDENT HARASSMENT

For Utah School, Lack of Policy on Abuse Yields Liability

Utah school officials are liable for failing to craft a policy that would have protected a disabled boy from being sexually molested by another student, a federal appeals court held.

Pointing to U.S. Supreme Court and state precedents, Judge William Holloway of the U.S. 10th Circuit Court of Appeals said the officials may be held liable for "violence committed by private actors ...where the state creates a dangerous situation or renders citizens vulnerable to danger."

Holloway affirmed a lower court ruling, which granted the school and the school principal 11th Amendment immunity from being sued for "endangering" a severely disabled boy who was abused in the school bathroom by another student.

The 14-year old boy, who has severe cerebral palsy and is totally blind and mute, used sign language to report the incidents to his mother.

Kathy Sutton testified that she was unsuccessful in persuading school officials that the incidents happened, and they continued until a teacher walked in on an older student molesting her 14-year old son, according to court records.

In the final incident, the teacher who was supposed to be monitoring the Sutton boy had stepped away for a few moments to answer a telephone, the records say. The student offender was later convicted of gross lewdness and forcible sexual assault.

The 11th Amendment protects state agencies from federal lawsuits in most cases, except when officials are found negligent when they abused their power. Both courts granted the immunity because they found that the principal did not "personally, affirmatively place [the boy] in any danger"—and because swift action was taken against the student offender once the abuse was discovered.

But the principal may be held professionally liable for failing to a craft policy that would have prevented further abuses once he learned of the first alleged molestation in February 1995, the judge said in reversing a lower court ruling dismissing a related liability claim against the principal.

"We are persuaded that [the allegations] cannot be dismissed as inadequate in light of the repeated notification to Moore ... of notice that [the boy], with all his impairments, had been subjected to repeated sexual assaults by the much larger boy," said Holloway, in delivering the opinion of the three-judge panel in *Sutton v. Utah State School for the Deaf and Blind* (97-4019).

"We are satisfied that a supervisor's liability for failing to train subordinates or to implement a policy to prevent a sexual assault on a severely disabled child ... was clearly established as of February 1995," he wrote in the March 1 ruling.

Kathy Sutton sued the school and the principal for violating her son's 14th Amendment rights to due process that included his right to attend school without being abused.

Holloway ordered the lower court to review the due process claim regarding the school principal's failure to craft policy preventing abuse.

Schools Can Be Liable for Peer Harassment

In a key decision for school distrcits, the Supreme Court ruled in May 1999 that schools can be required to pay victims of student-on-student sexual harassment if they knew about such incidents but failed to take disciplinary action.

The 5-4 decision resolves a split among federal appeals courts on the liability of schools under Title IX of the 1972 Education Amendments for sexual harassment among students.

The decision will have an impact on all schools that receive federal money.

In the high court's majority opinion, Justice Sandra Day O'Connor wrote that a school would be liable for peer harassment if the school knew of the harassment and remained deliberately indifferent.

"Deliberate indifference makes sense as a direct liability theory only where the recipient has the authority to take remedial action," O'Connor wrote.

She was joined by Justices John Paul Stevens, David Souter, Ruth Bader Ginsburg and Stephen Breyer.

Because the school can take disciplinary action against student sexual predators, the school has the authority to take remedial action, O'Connor reasoned.

Ruling Reversed

In 1993, Aurelia Davis sued Monroe County, Ga., school officials after she claimed Hubbard Elementary School failed to stop repeated harassment of her daughter LaShonda by a boy identified as G.F. in court papers. G.F. allegedly touched LaShonda's breasts repeatedly and propositioned her for sex.

In *Davis v. Monroe County Board of Education* (97-843), the 11th Circuit Court of Appeals ruled that the school was not liable under Title IX, prompting the litigants to challenge the case in the Supreme Court (SLN, Jan. 22).

That decision was similar to the one in *Bruneau v. South Kortright* (97-7495).

In that case, in which the 2nd Circuit Court of Appeals ruled in January that a school was not liable for the sexual harassment of a middle school girl, who had sued the school for failing to remedy a hostile education environment.

But in *University of Illinois, Urbana v. Doe* (96-3511), the 7th Circuit Court of Appeals ruled that the university, which operates a high school, was liable for damages against a girl who claimed that a group of boys repeatedly harassed her over a 17-month period. She claimed that, despite her repeated complaints, the school did nothing to remedy that behavior.

A High Legal Bar

In May 1999, the Supreme Court settled this question that has bedeviled the federal circuits. While schools are liable for damages in peer harassment cases, the bar for establishing harassment is very high and difficult to prove.

To start, litigants must show that the harassment was pervasive. Furthermore, schools must have been indifferent and aware of the harassment to be held liable.

This standard is almost identical to the one applied by the high court to sexual harassment by a teacher toward a student in *Gebser v. Lago Vista Independent School District* (96-1966). In that case, the court ruled in favor of the district because the school was unaware of a one-year affair between a teacher and student.

The high court sent *Davis* back to the lower court to determine the question of liability and what damages, if any, the school owes.

In his dissenting opinion, Justice Anthony Kennedy warned that similar suits would follow that would "impose serious burdens on school districts, the taxpayers who support them and the children they serve."

He was joined in his dissent by Chief Justice William Rehnquist and Justices Antonin Scalia and Clarence Thomas.

Bruce Hunter, chief lobbyist for the American Association of School Administrators, said this is a murky legal area, especially for incidents that occur in the early grades. "We will have some more first-graders disciplined for kissing first-grade girls as a result of this decision," Hunter said.

Davis Gives Boost to Sexual Harassment Cases

The Supreme Court's highly anticipated May 1999 decision on peer sexual harassment was a victory not only for the Georgia student who filed the hallmark case, but also for those with similar cases that are still winding through federal courts.

The high court's decision in *Davis v. Monroe County Board of Education* (97-843) says schools would be held liable for deliberately failing to stop "pervasive" peer sexual harassment. Attorneys for students say the opinion will force schools to take a closer look at the line between teasing and peer harassment, treating peer harassment as they would any attack on a student by a classmate.

Clear Standard of Behavior

"Ultimately, I think it serves the interests of children, parents and schools because now it is clear what standard of behavior is considered out of bounds," said Merrick Rossein, a New York attorney who is representing student Eve Bruneau in a sex harassment case.

"It's clear that schools have to take action as they would if one child punched another," he said. "[Peer harassment] is another form of hurting students."

Rossein in March appealed a 2nd Circuit Court of Appeals decision that affirmed two lower court opinions which absolved a New York school from liability for not stopping male classmates from sexually harassing Eve Bruneau. The high court agreed not to decide on whether to appeal the case until it had rendered its decision for *Davis*.

In light of the court's *Davis* action, the U.S. District Court for the Middle District of Tennessee is due to hear *Haines v. Metropolitan Government of Davidson County* (96-1085). Jessica Haines was a 10-year-old student when she said school officials were informed that boys sexually harassed her during school but did nothing to stop it.

The *Davis* ruling, which sets a national standard for what constitutes sexual harassment on school grounds, represented the ideological and legal split that has occurred nationally across federal circuits.

The 5-4 decision held that schools could be sued under Title IX of the 1972 Education Amendments and forced to pay students damages for failing to stop sexual harassment by students. The act bars gender discrimination at institutions receiving federal money.

Setting a high legal bar for such cases, Justice Sandra Day O'Connor wrote for the majority, saying that districts' liability should be limited to misconduct that is so "severe, pervasive, and objectively offensive" that students are precluded from benefiting from a public education. "It is not enough to show that a student has been 'teased' or 'called offensive names,'" wrote O'Connor, who was joined by Justices John Paul Stevens, David Souter, Ruth Bader Ginsburg and Stephen Breyer.

The dissent, led by Justice Anthony Kennedy, said the majority opinion would make school districts across the country financially liable for not settling schoolyard skirmishes. He was joined by Chief Justice William Rehnquist and Justices Antonin Scalia and Clarence Thomas.

The decision drew praise not only from lawyers representing students, but also from the National School Boards Association, which had argued with the Georgia district in *Davis* against school liability. "The standard is 'pervasive sexual harassment,'" said Julie Underwood, general counsel for the group. "If the court had left it at *all* sexual harassment, schools would be in a position where they would have to respond to even the slightest brush."

"Hopefully, the standard is high enough that we won't get the frivolous suspensions for holding hands or for kissing," she added, "because children are children. They are going to misbehave."

While some legal experts predict the decision will open the door to frivolous lawsuits even with the "pervasive" conduct standard, Norma Cantu, who heads the Education Department's Office for Civil Rights, said: "It is rare to find a school or college that does not respond, 'We want common sense.'"

Cantu said she expects all public institutions to continue their efforts "to prevent sexual harassment from occurring in the first place," and act promptly and appropriately. The *Davis* decision "neither imposes a national code of student conduct nor removes any needed flexibility from school officials' ability to maintain discipline."

William Taylor, a Washington, D.C.-based civil rights and education attorney, said the decision "sets a clear and fair standard that protects students and school districts." But he said the decision retains the same problem inherent in the Supreme Court's opinion in *Gebser v. Lago Vista Independent School District* (96-1966), which tied a school's liability in a sexual harassment case to whether the school was aware of the problem and still failed to act.

"That's troublesome because it discourages school districts from finding out, and it may discourage them from setting policy against such behavior or hinder students from succeeding in getting relief," he said.

Aurelia Davis sued Monroe County, Ga., in 1993 for failing to stop a student from repeatedly fondling her daughter and propositioning her for sex. The high court did not determine the amount of damages she should be awarded; instead, it sent the case back to the lower court to determine liability.

Colorado District Liable for Failing To Stop Sex Assaults

School officials in Colorado are liable under federal law for failing to stop a male student from repeatedly sexually assaulting a disabled classmate, a federal appeals court ruled in August.

Overturning key elements of a lower court decision in favor of Denver Public Schools, the 10th Circuit Court of Appeals found that school officials—despite their knowledge of "John Doe's" disciplinary problems—did not act to stop his repeated assaults on fellow special education student Penelope Jones.

Judge Stephanie Seymour of the 10th Circuit ruled that Denver officials "met Mr. Doe's sexually harassing conduct with deliberate indifference." Seymour, writing for a three-judge panel, found the school district liable under Title IX of the 1972 Education Amendments, which forbids discrimination on the basis of sex at public institutions.

The district failed the U.S. Supreme Court's test set to determine liability in such cases, the court ruled.

The high court in *Davis v. Monroe County Board of Education* (120 F.3d 1390; 1997) ruled that a school district may be held liable in sexual harassment cases involving students if officials are deliberately indifferent to the harassment, had knowledge of it, and the harassment is so "severe, pervasive and objectively offensive" that it deprives a student from benefiting from a public education.

Penelope Jones' mother, Penelope Murrell, sued the district on behalf of her daughter, claiming the Title IX violation and that school officials violated her daughter's 14th Amendment rights to equal protection by failing to provide her a safe environment.

The court ruled that Murrell had properly stated a case under Title IX and another much-used civil rights law that she used to sue individual school officials. But the court granted only the district, not the individual officials, immunity under that same civil rights law.

Penelope has spastic cerebral palsy, which impairs her ability to use and control her right side. She is also deaf in her left ear and developmentally disabled, functioning at a first-grade level.

Murrell told school officials that Penelope had been sexually assaulted at a previous school, expressing her fear that her daughter's physical and mental impediments would place her at continued risk.

In November 1998, school officials became aware of Doe's "aggressive and sexually inappropriate behavior" toward Jones. But they failed to stop Doe from sexually assaulting and beating Penelope, did not tell her mother about some of the sexual assaults, and encouraged her not to tell her mother, court records show.

Suicidal and engaging in self-destructive behavior, Penelope ultimately withdrew from school and entered a psychiatric hospital. At that time, her mother learned of the sexual assaults and beating Penelope sustained at school. When Penelope attempted to return to school in December 1993, Doe assaulted her again.

Jones repeatedly contacted school officials about Doe—who despite his history of severe disciplinary problems had a job as a janitor's assistant and access to unsupervised sections of the school building—but they failed to investigate the matter, discipline him or report the assaults to police, court records show.

The appeals court sent the case, *Murrell v. Denver Public Schools* (95-2882), back to the U.S. District Court for the District of Colorado to be reviewed.

New York Schools Not Liable in Peer-Harassment Case

New York schools officials did not violate a student's rights when they failed to remove her from a class in which she claimed boys sexually harassed her, a federal appeals court ruled in December 1999.

Claiming that school officials violated her rights under Title IX of the 1972 Education Amendments and the 14th Amendment, Eve Bruneau sued the South Kortright Central School District for failing to remedy a "hostile educational environment" in her sixth-grade classroom during the 1993-94 school year.

Title IX of the 1972 Education Amendments bars sex bias in federally funded programs. The 14th Amendment guarantees the right to due process.

The U.S. Second Circuit Court of Appeals unanimously upheld a lower court decision in *Bruneau v. South Kortright* (97-7495) that, though the boys' actions were "no doubt hurtful to those female students," the lower court was correct in ruling that the behavior did not constitute sexual harassment.

Eve claimed the boys regularly called her and her female classmates such names as "bitches" and "whores," shoved paper down their blouses and engaged in bra-snapping and hair-pulling.

Eve's mother recounted the incidents to a teacher, who assured her the behavior would not continue, and the teacher later testified that he did not consider the behavior sexual harassment. The boys denied the incidents but ultimately apologized to Eve.

Despite a "sexual harassment prevention" program instituted in the classroom, Eve said the boys continued their behavior. Her parents ultimately moved her to another school when school officials refused to transfer her from the class.

Though the Second Circuit affirmed Eve's right to sue the district, Bruneau's attorney, Merrick Rossein, said they will appeal to the Supreme Court the court's ruling that Eve had no constitutional grounds to sue the district for failing to train its personnel in sexual harassment prevention.

With courts divided in rulings across the circuits, it will be up to the U.S. Supreme Court to resolve the debate over whether school districts should be held liable in cases of peer sexual harassment.

Judge Richard Cardamone, in delivering the Dec. 31 decision of the three-judge panel, pointed to disparate rulings among the circuits on school liability. As an example, the U.S. Seventh Circuit Court of Appeals ruled last year in *Doe v. University of Illinois* (96-3511) that school officials may avoid liability if they "aggressively investigate" sexual harassment complaints.

But that ruling conflicts with decisions by two other federal appeals courts in the last several years that have found school districts legally blameless under Title IX for student peer harassment.

Washington, D.C.-based civil rights attorney William Taylor said the high court will have to settle this "terribly murky" issue of school liability. But the court's own rulings have been inconsistent, he said.

In 1998, the court ruled that school districts are not liable when teachers sexually harass students unless officials know and fail to act.

But the high court also ruled that Title VII of the 1964 Civil Rights Act protects employees from on-the-job sexual harassment by members of the same gender. The law prohibits gender bias in the workplace.

Court: School Not Liable in Sexual Harassment Case

Louisiana school officials did not violate a kindergartner's rights when they failed to stop a fellow student from sexually harassing him, a federal court has ruled.

The case involved a male kindergarten student who repeatedly exposed himself and made sexual gesture toward another male student at Pleasant Hill Elementary School in the Sabine Parish School District.

The parents of the victim—called John Doe— sued the district after the incidents persisted and school officials failed to respond, according to court records.

The Does said school officials refused to provide their "emotionally distressed" son counseling or act to stop the abuse—although the boy had been transferred to their son's class after he became sexually aggressive with other children and parents complained.

Title IX Violation?

School officials' failure to act violated the student's right under the 14th Amendment to attend school free from such abuse, the Does said. They also said school officials violated Title IX, which bars sex bias in federally funded programs.

But the ruling of the U.S. District Court for the Western District of

Louisiana disagreed with them on their 14th Amendment claim, citing previous Fifth Circuit rulings that favor public agencies in similar cases.

"A state's failure to protect an individual against private violence simply does not constitute a violation of the Due Process Clause," said Senior Judge Tom Stagg in the ruling.

The school district would be liable, however, if the parents could prove officials were aware they were creating a dangerous environment and they used their authority to "create an opportunity that would not otherwise have existed," according to the ruling.

The Fifth Circuit, covering Texas, Louisiana and Mississippi has shielded school districts from financial damages in a string of sex harassment cases.

High Court Snubs Review of New Harassment Case

The Supreme Court opted not to review a case that would have clarified whether a school district may be held liable for failing to stop student sexual harassment under a much-used federal civil rights law.

The high court in May 1999 ruled that school districts are to be held liable under Title IX of the 1972 Education Amendments if they know that a student is being harassed and fail to stop it. That decision addressed only suits brought under Title IX, not the separate civil rights law.

But the following month, the court without comment refused to review *Bruneau v. South Kortright Central School District* (98-1541), a case in which New York student Eve Bruneau accused South Kortright school officials of failing to stop male classmates from sexually harassing her during the 1993-94 school year. The court sent a separate case back to federal court.

Eve, who is now 15, and her mother say in court records that they repeatedly complained to school officials, who failed to respond and refused to transfer her to another classroom. Ultimately, she transferred to another school.

A federal appeals court in January 1999 ruled in favor of the school district and said that Congress intended for cases such as Bruneau's to be filed exclusively under Title IX, a federal law that bans gender discrimination at public institutions.

But Bruneau had already lost on her Title IX claim in federal court. Her attorney, Merrick Rossein, said he does not believe that Congress intended to block civil rights lawsuits when it enacted Title IX.

Lawyers for the school district say Eve should not be permitted to sue again because two courts have already ruled against her on the Title IX claim.

U.S. Court Says Michigan School Officials Immune in Sex Case

Michigan school officials were not notified of the repeated sexual molestation and rape of a mentally retarded girl by three of her male classmates, and therefore cannot be sued for damages, a federal appeals court has ruled.

Pointing to a recent Supreme Court case that set the standard for determining school district liability in these cases, a three-judge panel of the U.S. District Court for the Eastern District of Michigan ruled in favor of Huron Valley School District officials. The Nov. 2, 1999, ruling blocked the case from going to trial.

"[The school] did not have actual knowledge of the harassment until after the fact, and the plaintiffs have failed to present any evidence of deliberate indifference" on the part of the school, wrote Judge Eugene Siler for the 2-1 majority. "Once [school officials] did learn of the incidents, they quickly and effectively corrected the situation."

The Facts

In 1994, the girl, a Downs Syndrome child who functions at the level of a 7-year-old, attended Muir Middle School, taking a mix of special education and general education classes. Soon after starting school, she complained to her mother of boys kissing her and fondling her breasts and genitals.

Her mother asked school officials not to leave her with any of the boys accused of kissing or fondling her daughter. But the girl later reported being raped by two of the three boys she had accused of harassing her. Her mother again confronted school officials about the incidents and also reported them to police.

School officials then arranged to give the girl more supervision at school, including an escort.

They also installed windows in classroom doors, placed an aide in her classroom so her teacher would retain better control of the class, instituted a hall pass rule and placed an aide on the school bus. The three boys involved were required to attend student-counseling sessions on how to behave in socially appropriate ways with girls.

A police investigation resulted in one of the three boys being charged with rape. School officials suspended that student, but did not discipline the other two boys. While the police investigated the incident, the girl's mother kept her home because the boys were permitted to remain in school. But she returned to school in 1995.

Her mother then sued the district and school officials, claiming that they violated her daughter's rights under state and federal civil rights laws and under Title IX of the 1972 Education Amendments, which bans sex discrimination at federally funded institutions.

A lower court ruled that the district and officials properly claimed 11th Amendment immunity. The constitutional provision protects the government from lawsuits except in cases of gross negligence.

Judge Siler's majority agreed that the facts of the case (98-1550) do not point to gross negligence by school officials. The case also failed to meet two of three legal standards set by the U.S. Supreme Court's *Davis v. Monroe County Board of Education* (119 S. Ct. 1661; 1999).

While this case did reflect a level of harassment that was so "severe, pervasive and objectively offensive" that the girl was denied educational opportunity, school officials did not have knowledge of the incidents nor did they exhibit "deliberate indifference to the harassment," Siler said in applying the *Davis* standard.

But Judge Karen Nelson Moore—the dissenting vote on the panel—disagreed with the majority's ruling granting officials immunity from the lawsuit on civil rights grounds because she said it is not clear the officials acted to stop the harassment when the minor incidents were re-ported, let alone the eventual rapes.

"Whether their actions amounted to gross negligence is a question of fact for the jury," she wrote.

STAFF-ORIGINATED HARASSMENT

Elementary Teachers Lose Sexual Harassment Appeal

Sexually explicit letters mailed to two teachers' homes by a school prin-cipal did not amount to sexual harassment, a federal court ruled.

The U.S. Fifth Circuit Court of Appeals ruled against the two Texas teachers who sued their school district alleging the harassment.

Rose Butler and Erma Gracia were teachers at East Point Elementary School in the Ysleta Independent School District in El Paso, Texas, when they began receiving anonymous mail at their homes. A police investi-gation revealed that the sexually explicit letters were from school prin-cipal Kirk Irwin.

The teachers filed suit against the school district in the U.S. District Court for the Western District of Texas, but the court ultimately ruled against them. The Fifth Circuit upheld that decision in its opinion in *Butler, Gracia v. Ysleta Independent School District* (97-50362).

The Fifth Circuit rejected Butler's argument that the district was aware of Irwin's harassment of her since school officials already were investi-gating allegations that he faxed harassing letters to male administrators.

A jury initially awarded Gracia $35,000 in damages. But the court re-sponded to a motion by the school district and ruled that Gracia had no legal grounds because the letters were not "pervasive or severe as to cre-ate a hostile work environment [because] no harassment occurred at work."

The court also held that the harassment did not affect her employment and that Gracia failed to prove that the district failed to take "prompt remedial action."

Although the court recognized that the letters may have been unsettling, "the correspondence would not interfere unreasonably with a reasonable person's work performance," wrote Circuit Judge Patrick Higginbotham.

Gracia began receiving the letters in 1992 and brought the letters to Irwin when she suspected that a co-worker might have sent them, according to court records.

Irwin called an investigation, but never followed through, according to court records. In April 1993, Gracia discovered that Butler had also received letters and prank phone calls.

They began to suspect Irwin after they recognized patterns of his writing, such as misspelled words, in the letters. They reported the anonymous mail to the police in May 1993.

The district did not respond to Gracia's request to remove Irwin from the school. But after police matched fingerprints from the letters with Irwin's, he was suspended with pay. He retired in October 1993.

Florida School Officials Seek $1 Million Settlement in Sex Suits

Miami-Dade County school officials offered $1 million to settle two year-long lawsuits against a former high school principal accused of sexual harassment.

School attorneys negotiated a settlement of a half-million-dollar verdict awarded in federal district court to guidance counselor Jacqueline Hazel, who convinced a Miami-Dade civil jury that her boss, former principal William Clark III, sexually harassed her.

The district would have been responsible for paying Hazel a total of $900,000 once legal fees were added, but under the terms of the settlement she would receive $635,700, including legal fees.

Another lawsuit filed by Clark's former secretary, Sonja Miller, would be settled for $400,000.

The school board approved the settlements in February 2000.

Teacher Who Deemed Sex with Minors OK Has No Case

A federal appeals court has overturned a lower court jury verdict that favored a teacher who was fired because he testified in court that he has no problem having sex with minors.

Missouri's South Harrison School District voted not to review Phillip Padilla's contract after he testified in his criminal trial that teacher-student sex is acceptable. Padilla sued the board, claiming it violated his First Amendment rights by not renewing his contract on the basis of his trial testimony.

"It would be a strange regime that would permit a school board to be held subject to liability for failing to adopt and enforce a policy seeking to forbid and prevent teacher-student sexual contacts and yet at the same time be held subject to a suit for damages by a teacher" who finds teacher-student sex acceptable, ruled Judge Roger Wollman of the 8th Circuit Court of Appeals in June 1999.

Padilla, who did not appeal the three-judge ruling, was still in his probationary period when a female student told her classmates and a parent of her sexual encounters with Padilla.

The school board, in April 1993, initially found that Padilla had made sexually suggestive comments to the student, but found no evidence that he had sex with her. At the time, the board allowed Padilla—who started teaching in the district in August 1991—to continue teaching for the next academic year.

But several days before the April board decision, state prosecutors charged him with felony and misdemeanor sexual assault based on the information the student gave school officials and police. Padilla was acquitted in August of 1993.

But during his criminal trial he testified under questioning that teachers having sex with minor-students is acceptable "so long as the relationship is consensual ... and they're not in school or they're out of school."

In September 1993, the board sent Padilla a letter expressing their concern over his attitudes about sex between teachers and students. His attorney responded that the comments are protected under the First Amendment. Then in April of 1994, when the board was considering the contracts for all probationary teachers, the board voted not to renew his contract.

School officials told him in a letter that he was not rehired because a majority of the board believed he had "engaged in conduct prejudicial to the best interests of the school district by violating district policies with regard to sexual harassment and to relationships with students."

The board also made reference to Padilla's public testimony on teacher-student sex.

Wollman held that Padilla's First Amendment rights were not violated, "for it did not relate to a matter of public concern and it expressed no legitimate disagreement with the school board's policy vis-à-vis student sexual relationships."

"There may be other teachers across the land who agree with Padilla's views, but a court would be hard put to hold that the expression of those views would immunize a teacher from an adverse employment decision by a school board," he wrote in *Padilla v. South Harrison R-II School District* (98-1130).

GENDER ISSUES

SEX DISCRIMINATION

Court To Honor Society: Admit Teen Moms

The National Honor Society had to accept two teenage mothers who were denied membership last spring, a federal court ruled.

The U.S. District Court for the Eastern District of Kentucky says the seniors have a strong chance of proving that they were victims of sex discrimination and issued a temporary order for their membership.

Judge William Bertelsman agreed with the girls' argument that membership would not do "much good if they get admitted after they graduate from high school in May."

He ordered the honor society at Grant County High School in Williamstown to admit Somer Chipman and Chastity Glass. The school district complied with the order but will continue to defend itself in the lawsuit.

The honor society argues *Chipman v. Grant County School District* that "the public interest requires support of the public school's efforts to encourage high morals and strong character as part of the educational process."

ACLU Targeting Pregnancy Bias

Sara Mandelbaum, attorney for the American Civil Liberties Union's Women's Rights Project, says it will seek a permanent injunction.

"This should send a message to school districts that Title IX makes it clear that that kind of sex discrimination is forbidden," she said.

Title IX of the 1972 Education Amendments prohibits sex discrimination in federally funded education programs. It also makes it illegal to discriminate against a pregnant or parenting student.

Mandelbaum said the case sets an important precedent because "discrimination against pregnant or parenting students is widespread among school districts."

She says diverting teen parents from mainstream programs, for example, violates Title IX.

"Many of those practices are never challenged in court, but we will be pursuing them," said Mandelbaum, who works out of the ACLU's New York office.

A Small Town Prerogative

The National Honor Society sets national standards for its members but allows local chapters to create additional rules.

Students are selected based on scholarship, service, leadership and character. "It's the last three that they were found lacking in," said Suzanne Cassidy, one of the school district's attorneys. The reasons included school tardiness, lack of participation in school activities and their pregnancies, she said.

"Pregnancy was one of many factors, and it's allowed to be *a* factor," she said. "They were known in the community to be sexually active."

By the end of her junior year, Chipman had a 3.9 grade point average on a 4.0 scale. She gave birth in June to her daughter. Glass, whose daughter is 20 months old, has a 3.7 average.

GAY TEACHERS

California Bars Transfers from Gay Teacher's Classroom

Bakersfield school officials violated a science teacher's rights when they transferred 15 students from his class because he is gay, a California labor commissioner ruled.

Chief Deputy Labor Commissioner Jose Millan in March 1999 said state law prohibits employment discrimination based on sexual orientation—actual or perceived.

Millan wrote that Rio Bravo-Greeley Union School District officials "fostered different treatment in an aspect of employment based upon [Merrick's] perceived sexual orientation."

The ruling bans future transfers on the basis of eighth-grade science teacher James Merrick's actual or perceived sexual orientation, and forbids the school district from discriminating against him at all.

School officials began transferring the students from Merrick's class in September 1998. Parents at Rio Bravo-Greeley Union School learned that Merrick—in the summer—had announced his orientation while challenging a county official who made disparaging remarks about homosexuals at a hearing.

The parents reportedly complained of Merrick's mannerisms in class. In response to the transfers, Merrick filed a complaint with the state's Division of Labor Standards Enforcement and another with the school district, composed of a single, 800-student school.

School officials argued that they were not discriminating against Merrick, but were trying to appease the parents.

Millan said the district policy recognizes the importance of parental involvement in their children's education, but also said the district may not make placements simply based on a teacher's sexual orientation.

In this case, Millan said, the parents raised no other issue. He said the children should be returned to Merrick's classroom. Merrick, a 61-year old teacher of 40 years, is the school's only eighth-grade science teacher, so the transferred students were placed in study halls.

"It was never about money," said Myron Quon of the Lambda Legal Defense and Education Fund, the gay rights group representing Merrick. "It was always about the fact that what they did was wrong."

Lambda also is representing biology teacher Dawn Murray, who said officials at Oceanside Unified School District refused to discipline staffers who made homophobic comments to her at staff meetings. She also said they failed to stop other harassment that included vandalism of her classroom.

That case, *Dawn Murray v. Oceanside Unified School District* (D03662), was dismissed in California Superior Court, but is being appealed to the 4th Appellate District Court.

In November 1998, a federal judge in Utah barred a school district from prohibiting a lesbian teacher from speaking about her sexual orientation publicly (*Wendy Weaver v. Nebo School District*; 97-819).

CHAPTER 7

Mass Testing and Assessments

States riding the tide of high-stakes testing to improve student achievement may be vulnerable to discrimination lawsuits, experts warn.

All states embarking on mass testing face potential lawsuits based on sex and racial discrimination, due process, fairness and test validity, testing disabled students and adverse employment issues.

"High-stakes tests have aroused emotional debate in recent years, but more importantly they implicate a multitude of legal issues," wrote R. Craig Wood, a lawyer who speaks regularly at legal conferences. He noted that, in 1999, 26 states required students to pass high school exit exams before graduating; but in 1995 that number was seven.

He said the case law is limited, but the existing rulings—coming out of states such as Texas and Florida, which were among the first to institute testing programs—are instructive. The greatest legal risk is with states where testing is tied to consequences, such as not advancing to the next grade, or not graduating.

Legal experts say federal lawsuits in this area are usually filed under the Equal Protection Clause and Title VI of the Civil Rights Act of 1964, which requires the use of test materials that do not have a discriminatory impact.

"While it is difficult to show [or even envision] discriminatory intent in legislation requiring minimum competency standards in education, discriminatory impact is often a demonstrable result of such tests," Wood said in a paper written with attorney Dana T. Buckman, who works with

Wood at McGuire, Woods, Battle & Boothe. With women and minorities historically scoring lower than white males, many of the lawsuits arise from those groups.

Legal experts such as Wood note that courts usually defer to states and local school boards on academic standards. But "implementation of such high-stakes [tests] means that school system must be prepared to defeat potential litigation by preemptively ensuring their school reform not only is educationally valid, but legally sound," Wood said.

Schools Urged To Tread Cautiously in High-Stakes Testing

When school districts embark on sweeping education reform via high-stakes student testing, lofty achievement goals could lead to lawsuits, legal experts warn.

For example, a district may face defeat in court if it leaves inadequate time for students to prepare for a formal administration of the test, doesn't ensure that teachers teach the materials to be tested or if the test has an undue impact on a minority group, they said.

"The implementation of such high-stakes mechanisms means school systems must be prepared to defeat potential litigation by preemptively ensuring their school reform is not only educationally valid, but legally sound," said R. Craig Wood, a partner at McGuire, Woods, Battle & Boothe.

Speaking at the National School Boards Association Conference last year, Wood said the core legal complaints arising from high-stakes testing include racial and sexual discrimination, due process concerns, fundamental fairness and test validity, and the testing of disabled students.

The 10th Amendment gives states the "undisputed power" to educate their citizens, he said.

"The federal courts have been reluctant to interfere with a state's right to oversee education and will usually do so only when necessary to protect freedoms and privileges guaranteed by the United States Constitution," Wood said.

Wood and others pointed to cases from Florida and Texas, two states that have led the charge to high-stakes testing, that might help school attorneys predict legal outcomes. With females and minority students generally scoring lower on standardized tests than white males, discrimination claims in high-stakes testing are not surprising, he said.

The 1981 case *Debra P. v. Turlington* (644 F.2d 397, 402) arose after Florida passed legislation that set new graduation requirements for public schools. The first administration of the test resulted in 78 percent of black students failing; 25 percent of white students failed.

Black students filed a class-action suit challenging the exam, claiming it violated their 14th Amendment right to equal protection and due process; Title VI of the Civil Rights Acts of 1964, which bars race discrimination at institutions that receive public funds; and the Equal Educational Opportunities Act.

The 5th Circuit Court of Appeals agreed with a lower court that there was insufficient evidence to support a claim the school district intended to discriminate against the students. But the court upheld the district court's finding that the students are affected by "past, purposeful discrimination" and that the test and graduation requirement perpetuated that discrimination, Wood said.

The court barred the district from using the test for four years, except for remedial purposes. But four years later, the appeals court, by then renamed the 11th Circuit, revisited the issue and found the schools' remedial efforts for students help "severed the link between past discrimination and present disparate impact."

Ultimately, most of the failing students passed the test, and the court found that that proved the "vestiges of segregation do not cause blacks to fail the test."

It also said that denying a diploma to children who fail would help improve achievement for all students, thereby countering the effects of past segregation.

A Disparate Effect

If a testing requirement has a disparate effect on minorities, schools with histories of segregation will have to prove that the use of tests and the accompanying sanctions will help remedy that problem, Wood said. In the *Debra P.* case, the 11th Circuit court ruled that the testing schedule set by Florida officials violated the students' right to due process by giving students less than a year to prepare to pass the test or face not graduating.

The Texas case *Crump v. Gilmer* (797 F. Supp. 552, 554) shows how courts favor well-planned testing. A district court ordered a district to let two students—who had failed state tests by 2 points but met all other graduation requirements—participate in graduation ceremonies.

It said the students, who were graduating in 1992, only learned of the test 18 months earlier, when the state imposed the requirement.

"Schools should err on the side of being cautious, and those school systems engaged in high-stakes testing should allow time for students to prepare," Wood said, adding that time to offer students remedial programs and to correct any problem with the test should be included in any timeline.

A Fair Test

The *Debra P.* case also raised the issue of test fairness and validity.

"The court there held that if the exam covered materials not taught in schools, it was fundamentally unfair and a violation of both equal protection and due process," said Wood, who heads the litigation department at his Charlottesville, Va., law firm.

The court imposed a two-part test to determine test validity, Wood said. First, the test "must adequately correspond to the required curriculum in which students should have been instructed," he said. Second, the exam should correspond to what has been taught, regardless of what should have been taught.

Testing the Disabled

Wood said testing students with physical and mental disabilities can pose a special set of problems.

In *Brookhart v. Illinois State Board of Education* (697 F.2d 179,180), a group of students who had failed state competency tests for high school diplomas sued under Section 504 of the Rehabilitation Act of 1973.

The 7th Circuit ruled that altering the test for disabled students would be a "perversion of the testing requirement," but that a district failing to make modifications to the test format or the environment for students who are, for example, blind, would constitute discrimination.

Since disabled students have individualized education programs, the court said school districts must ensure that each child is exposed to most of the material appearing on the test or produce evidence that a child's educational needs are better met by focusing on goals that do not include preparing for the exam or earning a diploma.

High Court Refuses Review of Kentucky Testing Requirement

The U.S. Supreme Court has let stand a Kentucky appeals court decision that a school district's mandatory testing requirement is constitutional.

The state court had ruled that an assessment test administered by the Livingston County school board did not violate students' privacy rights or infringe on their constitutional right to the free exercise of religion. The nation's highest court in January refused to review the case.

But the state court also reversed an order from a lower court that had mandated the district to open the text of the exam to the public.

"We do not see that the exam advances or inhibits religion, nor that it fosters any government entanglement with religion," said state Judge Wilfrid Schroder, who delivered the ruling of the three-judge panel in *Triplett v. Livingston County Board of Education* (967 S.W.2d 25).

The parents of Chad and Tracey Triplett sued the school system after Chad was barred from graduating and Tracey from moving on to the ninth grade after refusing to take the tests. They claimed the mandatory testing requirement violated their constitutional rights to Privacy and to the free exercise of religion and their parental rights "to direct the education and upbringing of their children."

The Kentucky Instructional Results Information System tests are administered as part of statewide educational reform efforts to monitor school performance. Students are asked to answer some personal questions, such as whether they attended kindergarten. Test directions, however, note that they may decline to answer any question.

The court ruled that the tests' caveat protects student privacy, consistent with the Hatch Amendment to the Family Educational Rights and Privacy Act. The law protects students from being subject to inquiries on personal issues without due notice.

The judges found that the tests serve a secular purpose that doesn't violate the Establishment Clause of the U.S. Constitution. "We fail to see how they could be interpreted as attempting to promote or influence religious beliefs ... "The clause prohibits government from coercing citizens from participating in religion of any kind.

Texas Officials Charged with Altering Student Tests

In a case that underscores the pressure on schools to excel, a grand jury indicted the Austin school system and one district official for allegedly doctoring identification codes on some students' assessments.

Prosecutors in April 1999 obtained charges against Austin Deputy Superintendent Margaret Kay Psencik, saying she altered student codes on the Texas Assessment of Academic Skills (TAAS), and against the Austin Independent School District, which can be held liable for the criminal misconduct of its employees.

Psencik allegedly altered the student codes in 16 individual tests, deleting examples of poor results from the district's record and artificially inflating Austin's standings in statewide TAAS rankings, prosecutors claimed.

"This is not a happy day, but this action gives us the vehicle to try to correct the problems throughout the system which caused these types of violations," attorney Ken Oden said.

Oden conducted the test tampering investigation with the Travis County district attorney. Psencik's lawyer, however, denied the grand jury charges and vowed to seek a trial.

The Texas Education Agency (TEA) gives schools one of four rankings—exemplary, recognized, acceptable or low-performing—based in part on TAAS scores.

TEA awarded $2 million in cash awards to campuses showing better TAAS outcomes, providing nearly $50,000 to schools in Austin.

TEA detected discrepancies last summer and asked the district to investigate the case.

Although it has demoted ratings for three schools in Austin, it still gives the overall district an acceptable ranking.

"It's a very strong urban district," said Debbie Graves Ratcliffe, a TEA spokeswoman.

"They do a good job, and they've got many schools that are [ranked] exemplary or recognized."

High-Stakes Testing Conflict Misses Mark, Officials Say

Much of the conflict over high-stakes student testing is rooted in misunderstanding about what the tests should measure and how to use the results, a federal education official told the U.S. Commission on Civil Rights.

"There are many simple principles upon which many agree ... but too often people choose sides and not solutions," said Arthur Coleman, the Education Department's deputy assistant secretary for civil rights, at a June 1999 meeting in Washington, D.C.

"The testing issue shouldn't be about high standards *or* equal opportunity," he noted. "We can have both because good testing supports achievement and opportunity." But the issue has sparked heated debate and even lawsuits, as many states move to widespread testing of students to boost achievement.

Avoiding Legal Trouble

Critics are wary of such tests, they say, because of alleged test biases against minority and low-income groups.

In response to this, ED's Office for Civil Rights has been working since 1993 on a guide for a variety of high-stakes tests he says will help public schools avoid legal trouble. A draft of that document initially sent the education community into a panic over what some said was a rush by ED's civil rights office to publish a legal position that would discourage states from using widespread testing.

However, Coleman stressed that the guide, which is expected to be finalized by the fall, merely documents the cases and laws that govern such testing and said it is being crafted by OCR with input from the education community.

Who Needs Guidelines?

But one critic at the meeting questioned the need for guidelines, since school districts have attorneys who are in charge of keeping up with such issues.

"I'm not sure I understand the point of these guidelines," said Abigail Thernstrom, a member of the Massachusetts State Board of Education. "Every college has a general counsel, and we are cognizant of the case law of this discipline."

She said Coleman's interpretation of the guide as merely a helpful resource isn't consistent with the views of others who have read the document.

"There is much misunderstanding from both conservatives, like myself, and liberals on the position of this document, and OCR needs to clarify that misunderstanding," she said. "We believe OCR is presenting a biased view of the law aimed at discouraging testing."

"It seems to me OCR is saying use standardized testing, but only if you concede that the consequence of a low score is not the same for blacks and Hispanics as for whites," Thernstrom added. "They're saying get rid of high-stakes testing or race-norm your tests."

Coleman responded that he saw "no reference to race-norming" and added that the guidelines are very similar to a document OCR issued in 1997 to help states address student harassment and hate crimes.

Several commissioners questioned whether tests are necessary to ensure educational quality, given the problems with standardized testing and the disproportionate scores of minority students.

Nancy Cole, president of the Educational Testing Service, said standardized tests may be very useful in giving teachers another way to judge student progress. But "our fixation on tests misses the larger challenge," she said. "The real issue is the quality of education we are giving all our children."

Cole, who heads the nation's largest educational research and testing organization, was among the leaders who were leery of the OCR guide. After meetings with OCR, she said she is pleased with OCR's response.

She echoed the comments of several commissioners who pointed to the financial disparities among school districts and the difficulty many have with meeting high-stakes testing requirements.

"We don't need a debate that ignores the fact that our neediest students are now condemned to a second-rate education and dead-end jobs or unemployment," she said. "Fairness begins with the education we offer our children."

ACLU Files Suit Against California District over AP Courses

The American Civil Liberties Union filed a lawsuit alleging that California public high school students are being denied "adequate and equal" access to advanced courses.

"This first-of-its-kind case represents a compelling example of denial of equal educational opportunities in the aftermath of Proposition 209," the ACLU said in a news release. Proposition 209 is a state measure that bans racial preferences in education, hiring and contracting. The ACLU said the state has failed to assure equal access to advanced placement courses for students enrolled in lower-income, predominantly African-American and Latino schools.

The suit alleges there are limited AP course offerings in those schools. The AP program was developed by The College Board, a national educational organization that administers the SAT college exam, to allow qualified high school pupils to take college-level material.

Minnesota Court Affirms 'Zero' for Student Who Plagiarized

A school district did not violate the due process rights of a student by giving him a grade of zero for a project that he was found to have plagiarized.

"The record demonstrates the school district provided [the student] with substantial due process and its decision to affirm [his] zero grade was fair and reasonable," wrote Judge Daniel Foley for the Court of Appeals of Minnesota in *Zellman v. Independent School District No. 2758* (98-2313).

The student, identified as "M.Z.," asked the appeals court to review his case after the school board affirmed the findings and actions of the superintendent, principal and teacher in maintaining that M.Z. had plagiarized a book and therefore earned the failing grade.

M.Z. and his parents claimed the district had punished him too harshly in the 1997-98 school year because the assignment instructions were unclear. Students were required to explain events that took place during a decade in their own words, court papers say.

When M.Z.'s history teacher overheard students joking about photocopying pages of a book and turning them in to complete the assignment, she spoke to the class about plagiarism and stressed the terms of the assignment, the records say.

The school district maintains that all students are required to sign a student handbook, agreeing to ethical ways of behaving, at the beginning of the year. The guide defines plagiarism and indicates that students who plagiarize will receive a grade of zero.

"M.Z. has not demonstrated that he has a protected property or liberty interest affected by the charge against him of academic misconduct," Foley wrote for the three-judge panel in May 1999. "But even if he had established a protected interest, the school provided his claim with substantial due process and acted in an eminently fair and reasonable manner."

CHAPTER 8

Special Education

The most recent major development in this mammoth area of law came last year, when the U.S. Supreme Court settled the debate over whether school districts must provide professional nursing care to disabled students.

The case was *Cedar Rapids Community School Districts v. Garret.*

A key issue for school districts was whether they would be held liable for school clinic staff members who incorrectly performed health care tasks needed by some more severely disabled students.

The Iowa district sued by student Garret F. argued that the services he was requesting were exempted under the Individuals With Disabilities Education Act (IDEA) and that his parents were responsible for paying for them.

School districts around the country joined Cedar Rapids in expressing the fear that providing professional nursing services would strap already limited budgets. IDEA exempts school districts from paying for services that require a physician.

While the high court did not rule on whether schools could be held liable for the improperly performed health tasks of their workers, it did rule that school districts must provide for the health needs of the most disabled students.

The justices rejected the district's arguments regarding the expense, care and nature of the school district's services, instead holding that greater expense or complexity in services did not mean the services were barred by the IDEA.

A variety of other issues—such as student discipline and whether parents are entitled to attorneys' fees— keep the dockets full.

School attorneys describe the discipline section of IDEA as complicated and unclear.

But generally, disabled students are subject to the same restrictions and punishments as other students, with one rather big exception: If the student is determined to have acted out in violation of a school rule or policy as a result of his or her disability, no punishment or punitive action may be taken, attorneys' say. Instead, school officials must make adjustments to his or individual education plan.

But students have been expelled for, as an example, making threats against teachers when the outburst could not be linked to a disability.

Another much-litigated issue is whether parents or attorney/parents are entitled to receive attorney's fees when they represent the child. Essentially, courts have ruled—affirming the IDEA provision—that parents are entitled to "reasonable attorney's fees," but not if they opt to represent their own children.

High Court Ruling Means Schools Must Pay Disabled Students' Health Costs

School districts nationwide are required to pay for professional nurses to accompany some disabled students throughout the school day, the U.S. Supreme Court ruled last spring in a case with massive implications for local school budgets.

In the highly watched case, the court voted 7-2 that an Iowa school district is responsible for paying for the cost of continuous daily health care for an Iowa wheelchair-bound teenager. It said the federal Individuals with Disabilities Education Act requires one-on-one nursing care as a supplemental education service.

Cedar Rapids Community School District officials had argued that the nursing care they were being asked to provide Garret Frey, a 14-year high school sophomore who is a ventilator-dependent quadriplegic, was too complicated for school nursing staff and too expensive, since the district would have to hire a nurse.

The school officials said they consider the care Garret needs to be medical treatment requiring a physician, and IDEA exempts them from paying for those types of services. But a majority on the high court disagreed, affirming two lower court decisions ruling the services more worthy of a nurse, and telling the district to pay for it.

"This is a case about whether meaningful access to the public schools will be assured, not the level of education that a school must finance once access is attained," wrote Justice John Paul Stevens for the majority. "Under the statute, our precedent, and the purposes of the IDEA, the District must fund such 'related services' in order to help guarantee that students like Garret are integrated into public schools," he added.

IDEA requires that disabled children receive a "free and appropriate education." School districts are required to provide students with various "special education and related services" but not for medical services that would normally require a physician.

Garret, who Stevens called "a friendly, creative and intelligent young man," has been paralyzed from the neck down since his spinal cord was severed in a motorcycle accident when he was four.

The accident did not affect his ability to perform well in regular academic courses. But to attend those classes, he needs daily health care that includes urinary catheterizations, and a nurse to clear his tracheotomy, feed him, help him shift in his wheelchair, monitor his blood pressure and be familiar with the alarms on his ventilator.

Cedar Rapids officials estimated the cost of caring for Garret during the school day at between $30,000 and $40,000 annually. The decision could cost the district more than $285,000 in legal fees and nursing costs, however.

Justice Clarence Thomas, joined in his dissention by Justice Anthony Kennedy, said the majority's "broad interpretation" of the law—that cost is "irrelevant to the question [of] whether those services fall under the medical services exclusion"—will levy hefty fiscal burdens on states that Congress did not intend.

"This approach disregards the constitutionally mandated principles of construction applicable to [spending] legislation, and blindsides unwary states with fiscal obligations that they could not have anticipated,"

Thomas wrote in the case, *Cedar Rapids Community School District v. Garret F.* (96-1793).

Illinois School District Nets Loss after *Garret* Case

In light of last year's key Supreme Court ruling on student medical services, an Illinois school district has lost its bid to overturn a federal decision ordering it to hire a full-time nurse for a disabled student.

The Supreme Court's landmark March ruling in *Cedar Rapids Community School District v. Garret F.* (96-1987) held that school districts nationwide are required to pay for professional nurses to accompany some disabled students throughout the school day. The March 1999 decision carries major financial implications for districts nationwide.

The high court then refused to review *Morton Community Unit School District No. 709 v. J.M.* (97-3962), which in many ways mirrored *Garret*. Like the Iowa school officials in the *Garret* case, Illinois officials in *Morton* argued that the $20,000 a year needed to provide student "J.M." with a full-time nurse four hours a day for four days a week is not directly the issue. They said they are not required under the Individuals with Disabilities Education Act to pay for one-on-one nursing care for disabled students.

But the Education Department told school officials around the country to review students individually when deciding on the level of services a student needs. ED says IDEA excludes services provided by doctors, but not those provided by nurses.

The U.S. 7th Circuit Court of Appeals ruled against Morton school officials in July 1998, upholding a lower court's ruling that said supplying a full-time nurse is a "related service" necessary to meet IDEA's mandate that disabled students receive a free and appropriate education.

J.M., the 14-year old student in the *Morton* case, has birth defects that require him to breathe through a tube in his neck. He needs a nurse to monitor a portable ventilator and oxygen supply and to apply ointment to his eyes hourly because he cannot close them.

The Supreme Court's *Garret* decision—which affirmed an 8th Circuit

Court of Appeals decision requiring the Iowa district to pay for a student's nursing care—resolves major conflict among federal circuits.

Before *Morton* and *Garret*, three federal courts ruled that IDEA exempted school districts from paying for daily nursing care for disabled students:

- The 6th Circuit Court of Appeals ruled in 1996 in *Neely v. Rutherford County School* (68 F.3d 965) that continuous care to ensure a disabled student could breathe is a life-saving medical service not required under IDEA.

- The 9th Circuit Court of Appeals in 1990 ruled in *Clovis Unified School District v. California* (903 F.2d) 635 that IDEA excludes daily nursing care and that the law's exemption of certain medical services does not hinge on whether a doctor provides the care.

- The 2nd Circuit Court of Appeals in the 1987 case *Detsel v. Board of Education of Auburn* (9820 F.2d 587) ruled that nursing care for a child who needs a respirator is an excluded service under IDEA.

Iowa District Must Pay for Disabled Boy's Helper

An Iowa district is required to pay for a personal assistant for a disabled boy enrolled in a private school, but his parents are not entitled to reimbursement for legal costs, a federal appeals court ruled.

The Marion Independent School District was wrong in maintaining that Iowa law exempted it from providing special education services to students attending private schools, according to the ruling from the U.S. 8th Circuit Court of Appeals that overturned a lower court opinion.

"The school district's reading must be rejected because it would render nugatory [the law's] requirement that school districts 'shall make public school services ... available to children attending nonpublic schools in the same manner and to the same extent that they are provided to public school students,'" wrote Judge Frank Magill in the split April 1999 decision of *John T. et al v. Marion Independent School District* (98-2285).

"It would be nonsensical for the Iowa legislature to require school districts to provide services to a student 'attending' nonpublic schools and, in the next breath, to allow school districts to refuse such services solely on the basis of such attendance."

Magill said the statute "clearly mandates" that the school district provide services to students who attend private schools.

The family of Robert T., a student with cerebral palsy who voluntarily attends a private school, sued the district in 1997 when it refused to hire a full-time assistant for him to help him "meet the demands of his school routine" while he attends classes at St. Joseph Catholic School.

Though the family won favor from the appeals court on that issue, the court also said the district court erred when it ruled that the family's successful challenge under Iowa law constituted a win and entitlement to attorney fees under the Individuals with Disabilities Education Act (IDEA).

But the district court opted not to rule on the family's claim under IDEA because it held the family already had prevailed under state law.

The appeals court found that, since the district court failed to rule on the family's IDEA claims, the family was not entitled to reimbursement for attorney fees under that federal provision. The family may not have prevailed on its IDEA claim had the district court considered it, Magill said. Iowa state law does not support the awarding of attorney fees.

The appeals court ordered the case back to the U.S. District Court for the Northern District of Iowa to review the family's claim under IDEA and to determine whether the reimbursement of attorney fees would be appropriate. The court also asked the lower court to review whether the parents should be reimbursed for the cost of providing services to their son when the school district refused. Judge John Gibson agreed with the panel's decision to affirm the lower court ruling in favor of the district paying for services, but he disagreed that the family could only be awarded attorney fees if it prevailed under IDEA.

He said state statutes impose tougher requirements on the school district than those set by IDEA. Gibson said he would have affirmed the district court's ruling to award the family attorney fees under IDEA.

Because the claim already met the tougher standards of state law, the family should be awarded attorney fees under federal law, which allows states to set stiffer regulations as long as they are consistent with federal law, Gibson said.

IDEA does not require school districts to pay for private school tuition unless they fail to offer a disabled student an appropriate education in a public school.

School Lawyers Warn of Common IDEA Violations

Many school districts still are making decisions about the placement of disabled students outside the individualized education program (IEP) process, one of numerous lapses in conforming to the nation's special education law that leaves schools open to lawsuits.

School attorneys at the 1999 National School Boards Association's Council of School Attorneys seminar in San Francisco highlighted some of the more common, and often inadvertent, violations of the Individuals with Disabilities Act (IDEA).

Although many courts are taking a "no harm, no foul" approach when considering the effect of a procedural violation on a case, some legal missteps can spell instant defeat for schools.

In a number of cases—such as *Board of Education of the Hendrick Hudson Central School District v. Rowley* (458 U.S. 176, 201-06; 1982)—the Supreme Court has held that parents need to be integrally involved in everything from diagnosis to treatment of their disabled children.

The high court, in *Honig v. Doe* (484 U.S. 305; 1988), said parents should be involved in crafting IEPs because the plans set the goals for disabled children's education and are the "centerpiece of the statute's educational delivery system for disabled children."

Congress built into IDEA a number of safeguards to ensure that parents are not locked out of a process in which schools enjoy a natural advantage, experts said.

"The issue of what remedies are to be afforded parents for the commission of procedural violations in cases brought under the IDEA has been frequently addressed by courts," said Julie Weatherly, a partner at

Atlanta's Weatherly Law Firm who specializes in special education and anti-discrimination law.

"Several courts have found that procedural violations, in and of themselves, are sufficient to find a denial of free and appropriate public education to a disabled child," she said. Courts award relief typically when a violation has harmed the child, the parents or the child's education, she said. Weatherly spoke of 19 procedural violations that regularly spell legal disaster for schools:

1. **Predetermination of Placement:** School staff should avoid making final decisions on where a child is best served—for example, a neighborhood school or special center. Making hasty determinations outside the IEP process can violate a child's right to a "free and appropriate public education" as required by IDEA. Draft IEPs are acceptable, as is coming to an IEP meeting prepared to raise concerns.

2. **Setting Services Based on a School System's Available Resources:** "We just don't have the resources to give Johnny five hours of speech therapy a week" is not a legally adequate reason not to meet a child's individual needs. IDEA requires that a student's individual educational needs be met, regardless of available resources.

3. **Making Educational Recommendations Based on the Cost of Services:** The law does not consider the cost of services an adequate reason not to provide an educational resource. Only in limited cases can cost be a factor. Most recently, the Supreme Court ruled in favor of a disabled student from Cedar Rapids, Iowa, whose family argued that the school system should pay for daily nursing care while he attends school (ED, March 8). School officials argued the cost would be burdensome.

4. **Basing Decisions on Inadequate Evaluations:** School officials should ensure their evaluations of a disabled child are "up to date, thorough, adequate and appropriate before an IEP can be developed." It is difficult to defend a special education program when school officials fail to understand the level of disability they are charged with servicing.

5. **Failing To Be Clear on Why Regular Education Is Inappropriate:** Courts and federal agencies expect IEPs to clearly state why the IEP

committee—comprising special education and regular education teachers and parents—rejected the "least restrictive" environments, such as placement in a full-time regular education classroom.

6. **Being Overly Specific:** IEP are not substitutes for daily lesson plans. If it is written too specifically, Weatherly warned, school officials can violate the law by not following the IEP to the letter. Therefore school officials should know that parents are not entitled under the law to choose the teacher, curriculum, methodology or school site. But if it's written in the IEP, it may take a judge to change it.

7. **Failing To Offer Extended School-Year Services:** A school district's summer school program open to all students is not the same as extended school-year services for disabled children. School districts have lost cases in which parents have shown that extended-year services were not even considered in the IEP process.

8. **Taking Too Long To Craft or Offer an IEP:** When school officials are not prompt in developing and offering services for a disabled student, parents may seek those services from a private agency and successfully ask the school system to pay for it. IDEA gives school districts 30 days to develop an IEP after determining that a child is eligible for special education services.

9. **Improperly Constituted IEP Meetings:** The law requires all appropriate school system personnel, including a top-level school administrator and special education and regular education teachers, to attend IEP meetings. School principals or assistant principals should understand their supervisory roles in the disabled child's IEP planning.

10. **Barring People from IEP Meetings Brought by Parents:** The law allows parents to bring "knowledgeable" persons to IEP meetings. However, school districts may refuse to hold an IEP meeting if a parent spontaneously brings an attorney and the school system's attorney is not present. The school system may draw the line at the press or advocates who may hinder the IEP process.

11. **Failing To Notify Parents of All Who Will Attend an IEP Meeting:** A school system is required to give parents written notice of all who have been invited to the IEP meeting, including a school board attorney.

12. **Invalid Refusals To Allow Tape Recordings:** Parents often want to record meetings, and the law allows it. Generally, and particularly when a parent can show a true need to do so, school officials should allow taping. But the school system should tape the meetings separately for its own records.

13. **Lack of Clarity in the Amount of Services Offered in the IEP:** Parents have a legal right to know, clearly, what services will be offered—for example, three to five hours of speech therapy.

14. **Failing To Include Statements on Transition Activities:** By the time a student is 14, IDEA requires, as part of the IEP, a transition statement, detailing progress and goals achieved and to be achieved in areas determined by the IEP. This is a new requirement under IDEA's 1997 amendments and is often overlooked.

15. **Ignoring Students' Behavioral Management Needs:** If a student needs help improving general behavior, those plans should be part of the student's overall educational program, but not necessarily part of the IEP. "Functional behavior assessment and behavior intervention plans are the focus of the 1997 IDEA amendments, and it is clearly contemplated that these are to be conducted and implemented for students who are disruptive to the educational process for themselves or others," Weatherly said.

16. **Failing To Consider Graduation As a Change in Placement:** When a student graduates, the IEP team must meet in advance, giving appropriate notice of a meeting date to the system and parents. If a child receives a regular high school diploma, he or she is ineligible for further special education. But if the graduation is given under the special education department, the student is eligible for continued services.

17. **Failing To Consider an Independent Evaluation of a Disabled Child:** IDEA requires school districts to consider the results of outside evaluations of a disabled student. Although school officials are not required to act on any outside recommendation, they must consider it.

18. **Refusing Services of Any Kind without Written Notice:** School staff should never verbally deny services or make any changes in the "identification, evaluation or placement of a student."

19. **Giving in to Parents' Demands Even When Doing So Compromises the Child's Education:** School staff should not give in to the wishes of parents on the IEP. "It is clear that the right to a free and appropriate public education belongs to the child, not to the parents, and if school representatives truly believe that what the parent desires is not appropriate, the district may be required to initiate due process procedures" to ensure an appropriate education for the child, Weatherly said.

Study: Hearing Officers Key To Reducing Litigation

To cut down on special education lawsuits, Congress and states must make it more difficult for parents to challenge the findings of administrative hearing officers via litigation, a key study says.

An increasing number of parents and school districts are opting for lengthy and costly legal battles at the state and federal level to settle disputes over the education and placement of disabled students, rather than settling conflicts at the local level, the analysis says. But they need not do so, according to the findings, which were published in the summer 1999 issue of Exceptional Children, a research journal published by the Reston, Va.-based Council for Exceptional Children (CEC).

Less litigation would occur if it were harder for parents to challenge, in state or federal court, the decisions made by local due process administrators, said Quakertown, Pa., school district administrator James Newcomer, citing the report he co-authored with education litigation expert Perry Zirkel.

Not a Second Try

If going to court were not the next logical step in a special education spat, parents and districts would invest more energy and resources into settling disputes at the administrative stage—through mediation and other methods—instead of viewing litigation as a "second bite at the apple," the report said.

Keeping disputes focused on problem-solving at the local level would be desirable because the cost and length of such litigation often causes parents and school officials to lose sight "of the child's immediate education."

Congress has already acted on this tip, in 1997 amending the Individuals with Disabilities Education Act (IDEA) and requiring states to run voluntary mediation systems for parents and districts locked in special education disputes. And it retained the existing provision that compels parents to seek an impartial administrative hearing before filing an IDEA lawsuit.

Decisions made by local due process officers should be respected and not overturned by the courts unless the officers are "clearly erroneous," said Newcomer, who heads a special ed program in suburban Philadelphia.

Center Stage: Placement

Placement decisions have dominated special ed lawsuits, according to the Newcomer-Zirkel analysis of 414 published cases dating from January 1975 to March 1995.

Placement played the dominant role in two thirds (63 percent) of the cases, with parents seeking a more private and specialized setting for their child in 76 percent of those placement cases.

The study also found that:

- School districts, in cases that moved past the administrative process and into the federal courts, were predominately or completely victorious 52 percent of the time. Parents completely or partially won less than half, 41 percent, of those cases;

- On appeal to federal circuit courts, districts were winners in 60 percent of the cases, while parents were victorious 28 percent of the time;

- Districts scored predominant or complete victories in 53 percent of state court cases and 41 percent of state appeals court cases;

- Overall, at the conclusion of both federal and state court cases, districts were favored in nearly half (49 percent) of the decisions, parents were favored in 41 percent of the cases, and the remaining 10 percent of the decisions were split evenly; and

- While education litigation generally declined over the last two decades, special ed cases have become more frequent.

From 1990-1995, there were 613 published court decisions dealing with special education-related issues, compared with 515 cases from 1975, the year Congress passed IDEA's predecessor legislation, the Education of the Handicapped Act, P.L. 94-142.

There was one encouraging finding for parents. When courts overturn administrative decisions, the change tended to benefit the parents (63 percent of the time), not the districts (37 percent of the cases).

Congress, Newcomer and Zirkel concluded, should "mandate a uniform and more deferential standard of review when the IDEA is next amended." A uniform approach nationally would "encourage school districts and parents to accept the unlikelihood that courts would change or overturn ... results of the earlier administrative decisions," they said.

Also, Congress should improve the training of impartial due process hearing officers, ensuring "that the state administrative proceedings are increasingly fair to parents and school districts alike."

Money Helps

But increased deference to hearing officers is not the needed solution, according to Laura Rothstein, a professor at the University of Houston Law Center and a school litigation expert.

"A lot of it boils down to a [funding] issue," Rothstein said.

"There is too much litigation but it stems from a lack of resources rather than the parents having too many rights or having protections that go too far," she added.

But Zirkel disagrees. "You could say the same thing about general education as well ... that it too is under-funded," he said. "But why then has the number of general education cases dropped off?"

Changing Times

In the 1970's, there was a high number of education-related cases dealing with such volatile issues like racial integration and search and seizure, issues that are not as prominent today as they were then.

Special ed cases remain consistently "hot," Zirkel said, while general education issues, like sexual harassment, can produce a lot of cases in the short term but then peter out.

It wasn't until the 1980's that special ed cases began to pick up steam nationally, as the number of published cases increased by 600 percent over the previous decade.

In Pennsylvania, special ed cases are increasing at such a rapid rate, "we keep adding people at the administrative level just to keep up with it," Zirkel said.

"One of the ironies is that the better the system is in terms of accessibility, economically and the higher the quality of justice, more and more people will take advantage of it," he said.

Pennsylvania District Not Liable for Disabled Student's Tuition

A Pennsylvania school district is not legally required to reimburse the family of a transient disabled student who enrolled in private school after a disagreement over special ed services.

The boy's family, whose surname is not revealed in court records, sued the Radnor Township School District in 1998, saying the district violated his rights under the Individual with Disabilities Education Act (IDEA) and the 14th Amendment, which forbids states from restricting the basic rights of citizens. In this case, the family is accusing the school of violating their right to travel.

The Radnor school refused to accept an educational plan from the boy's previous Washington, D.C., school and wouldn't pay tuition at a private school after the family refused public school services.

"Radnor has done nothing to alter or deny [the student's] right, established by the IDEA and defined by state law, to a free, appropriate public education," wrote U.S. 3rd Circuit Judge Max Rosenn in the Jan. 14, 2000, opinion.

"It has not imposed different standards on the type of education [the student] may receive versus the type of education a disabled student who moves from one school district to another within Pennsylvania may receive," he wrote, for his three-judge panel.

The boy, who suffers from a learning disability and severe hemophilia, had moved to Pennsylvania from Washington D.C., where he had attended a private school and received educational services according to an individualized education plan (IEP).

In Pennsylvania, the family sought to use the boy's previous IEP and ultimately rejected the new educational options reviewed by public school officials. Radnor required that the then-17-year-old boy be evaluated according to Pennsylvania special ed policy to determine what services would best apply.

But the judge rejected the family's claim that the school violated the boy's civil rights: "Radnor's treatment of [the student] was not inconsistent with its treatment of Pennsylvania residents. Indeed, only by submitting to these procedures could [the state] determine if [the student] even had a right under IDEA to a private placement."

Rosenn continued, saying that the school took no illegal action by deciding, on an interim basis, that the boy was not entitled to attend a private school at the state's expense, especially since his father rejected several educational plans offered to his son.

The student "cannot claim that Radnor's action in this case violated his right to travel under the [14th Amendment]," he wrote in *Michael C. v. Radnor Township School District* (99-1124).

The family moved to New Jersey 41 days after arriving in Pennsylvania and subsequently sued Radnor.

Private Special Education Provider Didn't Violate Student's Rights

A private hospital, under a contract by a Connecticut school district to provide special education services to a nine-year-old boy, did not violate his right to an education when he was beaten up on a school bus headed to the facility, a federal court ruled.

The U.S. District Court for the district of Connecticut ruled that the boy's claims were baseless because Section 504 of the Rehabilitation Act and the Individuals with Disabilities Education Act (IDEA) do not allow individuals to sue for damages. The laws only allow for corrective action based on specific circumstances.

The Waterford (Conn.) Board of Education contracts with Elmcrest, a private partial hospitalization program, to provide special ed and related services to disabled services.

The district arranged for student A.W. to receive his special ed services at Elmcrest's facility.

After one week in the program, A.W. was attacked by several students on the school bus and needed emergency room treatment, according to court documents.

While the school district agreed to provide further special ed services to A.W. within its school system, the student's parents filed suit against Elmcrest claiming a violation of Section 504, the federal law that protects individuals from discrimination based on their disabilities.

The district court, in *A.W. v. the Marlborough Company and Portland Healthcare Inc.* (1998 WL 737875), said A.W. did not allege discrimination based on his disability, but instead challenges the adequacy of his free, appro-priate education, or FAPE, required by IDEA.

The court further stated that Elmcrest did not interfere with A.W.'s education. "To hold that this isolated episode resulted in a deprivation of A.W.'s [right to] special education would allow a student to bring a claim of this nature every time he gets into a school-yard scuffle," wrote Judge Alan Nevas.

Court Affirms Dismissal of Disabled Student's Suspension

A federal appeals court in May 1999 affirmed the suspension of a disabled student who was barred from school for violent outbursts against teachers and other students.

Betty Manning unsuccessfully appealed the opinion of a lower court ruling in favor of the Fairfax County School Board in Virginia. School officials suspended her son, Scot Manning, from St. John Davis Vocational Center for alleged repeated attacks on teachers, maintenance workers and other students.

Scot Manning, who is in his early 20s and received special education services from the center, was originally suspended in March 1993 for 10 days. The school then added three more days to the suspension after considering Manning's special needs and the safety of others at the center.

Manning was transferred from the center and sent to a residential facility, a placement to which his mother agreed.

But his mother sued the school system in district court, challenging the extension of her son's suspension beyond the original 10 days without an administrative hearing and noting that elements of his individualized educational program had not been carried out.

A district court ultimately thew out the case, granting the school system's motion to dismiss it. The U.S. 4th Circuit Court of Appeals agreed with the lower court in *Manning v. Fairfax County School Board* (96-1107).

Special Education Settlement Ends Dispute in Illinois

After a seven-year legal battle, a federal judge approved a settlement aimed at remedying what Illinois disability advocates claimed was a rampant practice of segregating disabled students in Chicago schools.

U.S. District Judge Robert Gettleman in June 1999 approved the settlement, in which the state school board agreed to pay $21 million over the next seven years to monitor Chicago schools and provide teacher education and planning in schools where disabled students have been segregated from other students.

In 1997, a federal court found the Illinois State Board of Education liable for failing to stop some schools from segregating disabled students from their general education peers.

Federal law requires schools receiving special education funds from the Education Department to include disabled children in regular programs to the greatest extent possible.

The 1997 ruling in *Corey H. et al. v. Board of Education City of Chicago* (92-3409) required the district to pay $24 million over eight years to integrate disabled students.

There are 430,000 students in the Chicago school district; about 53,000 of them are enrolled in special education. Under the settlement, the district's 583 schools will double their efforts to help disabled children reach academic standards and graduate.

Disabled Transfer Student Not Entitled to Transportation

An Iowa school district did not violate a severely disabled student's rights by refusing to provide her bus transportation when she opted to transfer to a new school, a federal appeals court ruled.

Judge Richard Kopf of the 8th Circuit Court of Appeals wrote in June that the family did not prove that the Cedar Rapids Community School District's transportation policy resulted in "disparate treatment" for "mobility-impaired students."

"We do not find a basis for concluding that the school district's [transportation policy] has a discriminatory impact upon the disabled," Kopf wrote.

Parents' Preference

In 1995, the parents of Kratisha H., a student with numerous severe disabilities, including cerebral palsy and spastic quadriplegia, asked school officials to transfer their daughter to a school outside her attendance area and pay for a specially equipped bus to transport her.

The family believed that transferring the disabled student to Kennedy High School from Thomas Jefferson High School would improve Kratisha's education.

The school district allows all students to apply for transfer to schools outside their attendance areas but requires them to pay for their own transportation.

Court records show the family does not contend that if Kratisha had remained at Thomas Jefferson, she would not have received a "free and appropriate education," as is required by federal law. Instead, the parents said it was their preference that Kratisha be transferred.

Given their daughter's disabilities, the family insisted the district pay for Kratisha's transportation. Officials refused to do so because they estimated the cost at $24,000 per year and there were no other children with moderate to severe disabilities who had similar transportation needs.

The family appealed to the Iowa Department of Education in 1995. An administrative law judge found in favor of the school district. The judge said the parent's preferences do not meet the legal criteria needed to compel the district to pay for transportation services.

The family then appealed to federal district court, which ruled that the district's refusal to pay for transportation services for Kratisha "limited her opportunity to participate in the benefits of the district's transfer program on the basis of her disability."

Ruling Reversed

But in May 1999, a three-judge panel of the 8th Circuit Court of Appeals unanimously overruled the lower court. "The school board's facially neutral transportation policy in its intra-district transfer program makes no distinction between students who will be required to provide their own transportation to their school of choice and those who will be transported by the school district on the basis of any trait that the disabled or severely disabled are less or more likely to possess," Kopf wrote in *Timothy H. et al. v. Cedar Rapids Community School District* (98-2723).

"Requiring the school district to spend any amount of money to provide transportation to students participating in its [transfer] program would fundamentally alter the main requirement of a program designed to be of no cost to the school district—parental transportation," he said.

"Establishment of a special bus route for a single student who admittedly receives a free and appropriate public education at her neighborhood school, but who wants to go to another school for reasons of parental preference, is an undue burden on the school district," Kopf wrote in reversing the ruling.

Attorney-Parents Not Due Fees in Special Education Legal Wins

Parents who are attorneys may opt to represent their children in special education lawsuits, but if they win, they are not entitled to collect fees, a federal appeals court ruled.

Pointing to legal precedent barring most plaintiffs who represent themselves from collecting attorneys' fees, the Fourth Circuit Court of Appeals ruled in December 1998 against a Baltimore, Md., parent, an attorney who represented his son in a dispute over his disability services.

"Loving parents ... will of course 'fight' for their children—with or without a statutory award of fees for their services, [but] to permit an attorney-parent to recover [fees] for representing his child is not necessary to ensure a parent's efforts on behalf of his child," Judge Frederick Motz wrote in delivering the unanimous opinion of the three-judge panel.

"But it might well lessen the chance that a disabled child would have the benefit of legal services from an independent party," Motz added in his Dec. 10 decision in *Erickson v. Board of Education of Baltimore County* (98-1075).

Paul and Mary Earl Erickson sought to have Baltimore school officials provide their son, Chase, with a special behavior modification program. A state hearing officer refused their request. They appealed to the Maryland Office of Administrative Hearing, which ruled in their favor and ordered the board to reimburse the Ericksons for costs associated with providing the program to their son.

When the board refused the order, Mr. Erickson, an attorney, filed a suit against the board, which ultimately agreed to reimburse the Ericksons

$10,421 for the program costs and $2,013 for expert witness fees during the administrative hearings.

But the U.S. District Court for the District of Maryland refused to grant Mr. Erickson attorneys' fees, saying the when an attorney represents his child in proceedings under the Individuals with Disabilities Education Act, the "congressional purpose" of IDEA is "best served by denying the award of fees."

The Ericksons based their claim on a "fee shifting" provision of IDEA that allows the court to award "reasonable attorneys' fees as part of the costs to parents or guardians" of a disabled child who prevails in a suit. But the Supreme Court and Fourth Circuit have ruled language in similar statutes were intended for independent counsel, the appeals court ruled.

"The IDEA fee-shifting provision should be read to encourage parents to obtain independent legal services," Motz wrote.

Although Mr. Erickson obtained an "excellent result" for his son, Motz said his inexperience resulted in missed filing deadlines that ran up the extra court costs.

"This case illustrates the difficulties of encouraging inexperienced attorney-parents, via a statutory fee award, to represent their own children in IDEA proceedings," Motz said.

No Fees for Attorney-Parents in Disability Cases

The Supreme Court last June refused to review a case that would have determined whether parents who are attorneys are entitled to collect fees when they successfully represent their disabled children.

The court let stand, without comment, the 4th Circuit Court of Appeals ruling in *Doe v. Baltimore City Board of Education* (98-1613), which held that an attorney-parent who represents a child is not entitled to collect fees. The ruling will only affect cases in the 4th Circuit states of Maryland, North Carolina, South Carolina, Virginia and West Virginia.

The 4th Circuit Court of Appeals on Dec. 10, 1998, affirmed a lower court ruling that John Doe, who represented his autistic son, is not entitled to attorney fees, pointing to a number of precedents. One key case is the Supreme Court's 1991 *Kay v. Ehrler* (499 U.S 432; 111 S. Ct. 1435), which bars an attorney who self-represents from being awarded attorney fees, wrote Judge Diane Gribbon Motz for the three-judge panel.

But under the Individuals with Disabilities Education Act (IDEA), families with independent lawyers may be awarded "reasonable" legal fees as part of the costs to the parents or guardian of a disabled child, at the court's discretion. However, IDEA does not allow parents who represent their children to be awarded attorney fees because the result could be children who are represented by inadequate counsel, she wrote.

"Loving parents, like the Does, will of course 'fight' for their children—with or without a statutory award of fees for their services," Motz wrote. "To permit an attorney-parent to recover statutory fees for representing his child in IDEA proceedings is thus not necessary to ensure a parent's efforts on behalf of his child."

Not encouraging third-party attorneys for disabled children would "'compound' the child's handicap simply because his parent is an attorney," she said.

"Precisely because disabled children deserve independent legal services, the IDEA fee-shifting provision should be read to encourage parents to obtain independent legal services."

But the 4th Circuit court also agreed with the lower court ruling that awarded the family the cost of providing expert witnesses during the trial and the cost of providing a special education program to their son. Those costs totaled more than $12,400.

The Does sued the school district last year after officials refused to pay for a specialized program found to be effective in improving the skills of autistic children. The family was unsuccessful in seeking relief from one state agency, but an appeals panel of the Maryland Office of Administrative Hearings ruled that the school district should reimburse the family for fees associated with providing the program to their son. The parents sued the district in federal district court to recover attorney fees but were unsuccessful.

The 3rd Circuit Court of Appeals last December ruled that parents who are not attorneys may represent their children in administrative hearings but not federal court.

IDEA Rules Weaken Stance on Awarding Attorney Fees

Revising an earlier stance, rules for the nation's special education law do not encourage states to let hearing officers award attorney fees to parents who prevail in disputes with school districts.

The Education Department, in its final regulations for the updated Individuals with Disabilities Education Act (IDEA), deleted a footnote from its proposed rules which mentioned that states can grant the extra power over legal costs to independent officers who preside over administrative hearings in special ed spats.

ED sparked criticism of its proposed rules in late 1997 by suggesting that states allow hearing officers to penalize schools when parents prevail in special education disputes.

The final regulations to IDEA, released in March 1999, do not address the subject, reserving an explanation for the "commentary" section of the document.

Just a Suggestion

ED's commentary on the final rules says "the proposed note was merely intended to suggest that states could choose as a matter of state law to permit hearing officers to award attorneys' fees to parents and not require that they do so, or imply that IDEA would be the source of the authority for granting hearing officers that role."

ED's special ed chief, Judith Heumann, confirmed the issue remains a state prerogative, saying individual states must decide whether to allow hearing officers to award attorneys' fees.

Perry Zirkel, a professor at the University of Idaho and an expert on special education law, interpreted ED's decision not to incorporate the attorneys' fees footnote into the final regulations as an olive branch to congressional Republicans.

An objective person might conclude that, by removing its proposed footnote, ED no longer interprets IDEA to address the question about hearing officers and legal fees, Zirkel added.

The final rules incorporate some of the 126 footnotes that appeared in the proposed regulations, and delete others. Some school administrators complained that the notes were confusing.

IDEA requires parents to take their complaints to administrative hearings before going to court, but the law does not specify that hearing officers can award money. Instead, IDEA authorizes federal district courts to award "reasonable attorneys' fees" to the parents when they win a case.

The awarding of fees in special ed cases has been an ongoing issue for school administrators throughout the nation. An Iowa school district, for instance, recently lost a court case involving a disabled student who needs daily nursing care, and now expects to pay $500,000 in legal fees and health care expenses.

Education Department Would Force Schools To Serve Expelled Kids

Surprising advocates for schools, the Clinton administration has proposed requiring schools to finance all needed academic and counseling services for students who have been suspended or expelled from school.

The proposal—which would extend an existing assurance for disabled children to virtually all 53 million regular education students in the United States—appears in Title XI of President Clinton's bill to update and revise the 1965 Elementary and Secondary Education Act (ESEA).

Congress is expected to act on the revisions this fall. Aiming to keep students who have been suspended or expelled involved in academics, section 11206 of the Clinton bill would require school districts to provide such children with "appropriate supervision, counseling, and educational services that will help those students continue to meet the state's challenging standards."

William Modzeleski, director of the Education Department's safe and drug-free schools program, said the president advanced this discipline plan for two reasons: to ensure that disruptive children have a realistic opportunity to meet academic standards when they return to regular classes, and to prevent juvenile crime.

Children suspended or expelled to the street without any interventions "become more likely to become engaged in illegal and illicit activities," Modzeleski said.

Congress already has enacted a similar provision in the controversial Individuals with Disabilities Education Act (IDEA), which lawmakers revised in 1997.

IDEA requires schools to provide services to all special education students, "including children with disabilities who have been suspended or expelled from school." That language overturned a key decision from the U.S. 4th Circuit Court of Appeals, which had allowed Virginia to cut off services to disabled children ejected from class for bad behavior.

Furthermore, the administration's ESEA plan echoes a recent debate in Congress. The Senate last year passed an amendment by Sen. Tom Harkin, D-Iowa, that would require schools to provide at least mental health services to all children suspended or expelled from classes.

But the Senate revealed its own mixed feelings on the issue, passing a GOP amendment that would let schools cut off services to disabled children who bring guns or bombs to school. Many Democrats voted for that amendment, which passed, 75-24.

President Clinton at first only dropped hints about his discipline goals, asking Congress in January 1999 to require schools to adopt "sensible" approaches. With the details out, the administration is gaining support from its allies, including the National Education Association (NEA).

Clinton's bill is "not inconsistent with where we are, because, clearly, the last thing you want are kids running around on the street," said Diane Schust, an NEA lobbyist. The group last July passed a resolution calling for schools to remove from class all violent students, disabled or not, and enroll them in viable alternative programs.

Larry Sullivan, a lobbyist for the National Association of School Psychologists, gave a preliminary nod of approval to the administration for trying to maintain educational and counseling services to troubled youths. "It really brings us to one standard, not to give up on these kids," he said. "That's what I want."

Without endorsing Clinton's plan, researchers have laid a strong foundation for his proposal, claiming that truant and expelled youth commit a large proportion of daytime burglaries.

School groups want to run alternative programs but fret about costs.

Michael Resnick, associate director for advocacy and issues management at the National School Boards Association, noted that the president has not tied his new discipline policy to any new funding stream. "You can sit in your ivory tower somewhere and concoct a nice strategy, and we can all say that's a nice goal," he said. "But in practice, it's the kind of mandate that would be difficult to achieve."

Bruce Hunter, lobbyist for the American Association of School Administrators, called the administration's school discipline plan "the largest unfunded mandate since IDEA."

"There's no pretense of funding here," Hunter said. "There's just the mandate, with no help."

Modzeleski retorts that the administration's overall K-12 approach, including smaller classes and funding for after-school programs, can help prevent discipline woes.

House Republicans are determined to ensure that federal policies do not override state or local school discipline laws. "We have heard from a lot of educators about this provision, and we will be taking a very careful look at it," said Vic Klatt, education policy coordinator for the House Education and the Workforce Committee. "It raises a host of issues that our members will want to examine before going forward."

Connecticut Teachers Balk At Restraining Students

A Connecticut arbitration panel has overruled a controversial decision that could have radically altered the way state schools deal with disruptive disabled students.

The 200-member teacher's union in Clinton, a New Haven suburb, is renegotiating its contract with the state, seeking to exclude a new requirement that teachers physically restrain students.

School officials, however, have resisted, saying it would be too costly to assign such tasks to security officers and others.

Both sides agreed to arbitration.

Paul Mohor, a seventh-grade math teacher and a certified special ed instructor, said the union pursued the clarification after reading in IEPs that teachers would be required to physically restrain students. "Maybe some teachers wouldn't feel comfortable doing this."

Court Says ADA Doesn't Cover Test Angst

The 10th Circuit Court of Appeals last year ruled that a graduate student suffering from test anxiety is not covered under the nation's disabilities law.

The court said Kevin McGuinness, a medical student at the University of New Mexico, could not file for damages against the school for violating his rights under the Americans with Disabilities Act (ADA).

ADA states that no qualified individual with a disability can be denied services from a public entity. But the law also defines disability loosely, as an impairment that "substantially limits one or more of the major life activities," leaving the courts to further hone the definition of "major life activity."

In *Kevin M. McGuinness v. University of New Mexico School of Medicine*, the courts relied on regulations from the Equal Employment Opportunities Commission (EEOC), which cite numerous examples, such as caring for oneself, walking, breathing, learning, and walking.

When considering whether McGuiness's test- taking anxiety constituted a serious impediment to a "major life activity," the court used three criteria. These include its nature and severity; its duration; and whether it is permanent or long-term.

Court Rejects LD Waiver on Minnesota Test Requirement

A federal district court in Minnesota has ruled against a teacher who sought a waiver from the math portion of the state's licensure exam because of a learning disability.

In *Jacobson v. Tillman* (97-1541), the U.S. District Court for the District of Minnesota ruled that Judy Jacobsen did not qualify for a waiver under the Americans with Disabilities Act and that the court would defer to the Minnesota Board of Teaching on its selection of standardized tests.

Jacobsen, a trained elementary teacher who has taught with a temporary license in both private and public schools, failed the math portion of the state exam 13 times.

In asking the state board for a waiver, she claimed the failures were caused by her dyslexia, which impairs her ability to read, spell and write words, and dyscalculia, or an impaired ability to perform math problems due to brain injury or disease.

The state board repeatedly told her it had no legislative authority to grant an alternative testing format, but Jacobsen said the board violated Title II of ADA, which forbids "qualified individuals" from being denied opportunities because they are disabled.

Before the matter went to trial, the court ruled in favor of the board, saying the test is "an essential eligibility requirement for licensure."

CHAPTER 9

Substance Abuse

Federal courts in recent years have begun to uphold school districts' drug-testing policies as long as they are limited to a select group of individuals, such as school athletes, and are considered to be in the interest of student safety.

Legal experts say that before 1995, student drug-testing programs rarely prevailed in the courts, with rulings deeming them a violation of the Fourth Amendment's ban against unreasonable search.

But the high court's 1995 ruling in *Vernonia School District v. Acton* (515 U.S. 646) held legal a drug-testing program allowing random urinalysis testing of student athletes without the reasonable suspicion standard the court established in *New Jersey v. T.L.O.*

Essentially, the high court ruled that requiring student athletes to submit to random urinalysis testing was reasonable because:

- There is a lower expectation of privacy for public school students;

- Public school officials have "substantial authority" over student behavior;

- Students, and especially athletes, are already required to submit to various physical examinations and vaccines;

- Students agree to higher oversight by joining athletic teams, and the risk of injury is greater when students are under the influence; and

159

- School officials have a "compelling interest" in protecting students from illegal drugs and alcohol.

More recent federal rulings have reflected a judicial tolerance for limited testing. For example, the Colorado Supreme Court in 1998 rejected a school district's policy of testing all students in sixth- through 12th-grade who want to participate in extracurricular activities. A student band member challenged the policy, and won.

The court ruled it was too broad because it included students enrolled in credit-classes such as band, as well as after-school sports. The court also ruled that the physical risk to student athletes using drugs was greater than that for band members.

The high court let stand a 7th Circuit Court of Appeals ruling in *Todd v. Rush County Schools* (133 F.3d 984) that allowed testing of students participating in extracurricular activities. In that case, the 7th Circuit Court Appeals found similarities between that policy and the Vernonia one in that its aim was to "deter drug use and not...catch and punish users."

John Murry, Jr., associate professor of higher education at the University of Arkansas, recommends that school districts do the following to craft policies that will pass legal muster:

- Evaluate the need for a drug testing policy, include documentation of a drug problem, and query school staff and community for their support;

- Determine the necessary level of testing, i.e. frequency, how many students per sports, which student athletes, cost to the school or students, and whether students will be required to disclose pre-existing medical conditions and medications taken;

- Determine whether testing will be random or mandatory, and ensure objectivity in random testing; and

- Determine how the samples will be processed; consider student privacy issues, mechanisms for handling students who refuse to take the test, any necessary staff training and who has access to the test results.

He stressed that, at a minimum, policies should have a data-based rationale, procedural guidelines and individualized testing, as opposed to mass testing.

DRUG TESTING

Vernonia Principal Urges Limited Drug Testing

Public schools should shy away from implementing comprehensive drug testing programs and instead focus on testing student athletes, says a pioneering principal.

"There doesn't seem to be a compelling interest yet" to test all public school students, said Randall Aultman, former principal of Vernonia (Ore.) High School, which implemented the nation's first student athlete drug test in 1989.

There is "something special" in protecting the safety of student athletes, Aultman said at the 1999 regional drug testing conference in Arlington, Va., sponsored by American Bio Medica. He added that athletes on drugs are more apt to injure themselves or others while playing.

Currently, public schools may test student athletes if they can show it's in the best interest of student safety. In 1995, the U.S. Supreme Court upheld Vernonia's policy in *Vernonia v. Acton* (115 S. Ct. 2386).

And the High Court has been paving the way for a possible national expansion of comprehensive student drug testing. Last month, the High Court upheld an Indiana school district's policy to test all students involved in extra-curricular activities, whether they be baseball players or chess club members.

Presumption of Guilt?

But such policies have plenty of critics.

Random testing "treats all students as if they are guilty, and forces them to prove their innocence," which is the opposite of what the Fourth

Amendment was designed for, said David Fidanque, executive director of Oregon's chapter of the American Civil Liberties Union.

"The message that random testing sends to good kids is that it doesn't matter how you behave, you are still a suspect," he said. "In the long term, it breeds contempt, not respect for authority."

More Rural Testing

Student athlete drug testing is performed far more often at small, rural schools rather than larger urban districts, Aultman said. Vernonia High School, located in a rural logging community in northwest Oregon, has 200 students.

There is "not as much bureaucracy" in the smaller districts, and there are "more lawyers available in the larger schools," said Aultman. "The more lawyers available, the less likely drug testing is going to be enacted."

Big school districts "have their heads in the sands," said Ron Slinger, a former athletic director and current teacher at a Dixon, Calif., high school.

"It's easier to ignore the problem than to combat it," said Dixon, whose school is located about 20 miles outside Sacramento and has a student population of roughly 1,000.

Fidanque agrees that for many school administrators, "solving problems is much less important than making it look like they're dealing with a problem." School administrators "tend to grasp at easy solutions that may or may not work," he said.

The Formula

But schools should not face any future legal squabbles if they follow the formula in place at Dixon and Vernonia, Aultman and Slinger said. They suggested that:

- All student athletes be tested before the start of the season, with random testing performed throughout the season;

- Peer counseling programs be conducted through the athletic department;

- Every athletic program hold at least one drug education meeting per season;

- A task force comprised of the athletic director, coaches, teachers outside of the athletic department, school board members, students and community members should determine a school's drug testing policy and mission statement; and

- The athletic director should be in charge of the drug testing program.

Aultman began drug testing student athletes at Vernonia in 1989, but was temporarily barred from continuing the practice after the parents of of a seventh-grader filed a lawsuit.

When the Supreme Court took up *Vernonia v. Acton*, it ruled that deterring drug use among high school athletes with random drug testing served a "compelling interest to protect the health of the students."

But the 1992 lawsuit, filed by the family of then-12-year-old James Acton and funded by the ACLU, dragged the school district through the courts for three years.

Voluntary testing was performed during the months between a Ninth District U.S. Appeals Court found that the Vernonia policy violated Acton's Fourth Amendment right to privacy and the Supreme Court's overturning of that decision.

While the Vernonia decision was a major setback, it wasn't unexpected, Fidanque said.

The Court "has not been well-disposed to search and seizure claims whether made by innocent or guilty people," he said.

This is not the first time the Court has ruled on Fourth Amendment privacy issues. In 1989, the Court ruled in *Skinner v. Railway Labor Executives Association* (489 U.S. 602) that the government's "special need" for safety sometimes outweighs an employee's right to privacy.

Court: Widespread Student Drug Test Unconstitutional

An Indiana school district's policy to drug test all students who are suspended, no matter what the offense, is unconstitutional, the U.S. Seventh Circuit Court of Appeals ruled last year.

The court, in *Willis v. Anderson Community School Corporation* (98-1227), said the school district's policy was too vague and tested students who were not suspected of using drugs, a violation of the Fourth Amendment which prohibits unreasonable government searches.

"The imposition of a suspicionless policy seems to serve primarily demonstrative or symbolic purposes," wrote Judge Richard Cudahy.

Court Clarifies Terms

The main distinction between this case, and an earlier ruling by this court in favor of a school's drug testing policy, is the types of students tested.

The case focused on James Willis, an Anderson High School freshman suspended for three days for fighting. The school makes no distinction between who initiates the fight, and all involved get suspended.

In *Todd v. Rush County Schools* (133 F.3d 984), the Seventh Circuit had ruled that a Rush, Ind., school district could legally require drug tests of all students participating in extra-curricular activities.

Both decisions were based on whether students voluntarily participated in a school activity, said Kenneth Falk, an attorney for the Indiana Civil Liberties Union who represents the students in both cases.

"The court took a common sense approach by saying that going out for the chess club is different than getting into a fight," Falk said in an interview Thursday. He is appealing the Seventh Circuit's ruling in *Todd* to the U.S. Supreme Court.

The Seventh Circuit also cited a June 1999 Colorado Supreme Court ruling that said a school district cannot force junior high and high school band members to submit to urinalysis drug testing because it constitutes an unreasonable search. The court said that since students take a band class for credit, in addition to the extra-curricular nature of the marching band, students couldn't be compelled to be tested.

The Anderson Community School Corporation argued that students get into fights voluntarily, therefore the policy was legal. But the Seventh Circuit called that argument "strained."

Broad Policy

The school district's policy mandates a drug and alcohol test for any student who: possesses or uses tobacco; is suspended for three days or more for fighting; is truant; or violates any other school rule that results in a three-day suspension.

While students don't receive extra punishment if the drug test is positive, they may be expelled if they don't participate in a drug awareness program.

Students who refuse to be tested are considered to have admitted to drug use.

The policy was based on research that says students who fight, sleep more than usual, or defy rules may potentially be using drugs. The research cautioned that many teenagers exhibit some form of this behavior even if they aren't using drugs.

"We cannot find that the [school district's] data is strong enough to conclusively establish reasonable suspicion of substance abuse when a student is suspended for fighting," Cudahy wrote.

The court cited a 1995 U.S. Supreme Court ruling in *Vernonia v. Acton* (115 S.Ct.2386) in which the High Court determined that deterring drug use among high school athletes with random drug testing served a "compelling interest".

But in that case, the Seventh Circuit said, there was reasonable suspicion that the athletes were doing drugs and that they voluntarily participated in school sports.

Falk said the school district could make its policy pass constitutional muster by requiring school administrators to evaluate students when they are suspended.

Colorado Top Court Bans Student Drug Testing

A school district cannot force junior high and high school band members to submit to urinalysis drug testing because it violates their constitutional rights, the Colorado Supreme Court ruled last July.

Since students in the high school band must take courses for graduation credit to participate, the court said students' participation in the extracurricular activity is not entirely voluntary.

The Trinidad School District drug testing policy wrongfully included students in for-credit courses and students who had not shown they had contributed to the district's drug problem. The district also didn't show that there was a risk of physical harm to members of the marching band, according to Colorado Supreme Court Justice Mary Mullarkey, who authored the majority's opinion in *Trinidad School District No. 1 v. Carlos Lopez* (97SC124).

The court relied heavily on the U.S. Supreme Court's 1995 opinion in *Vernonia v. Acton* (115 S. Ct. 2386), which said deterring drug use among high school athletes with random drug-testing served a "compelling interest".

The Colorado court looked at a three-part test used by the U.S. Supreme Court to justify student drug testing. The High Court considered:

• a student's expectation of privacy;

• the character of the drug test; and

• the government's, or school's, reasons for instituting drug testing.

Colorado's Supreme Court said that in *Vernonia,* student athletes have a lesser expectation of privacy because they volunteer for sports teams and participate in "communal undress" by changing clothes and showering in front of each other. "We view the absence of voluntariness and the qualitatively different type of undressing in this case as significant," Mullarkey wrote.

Trinidad School District's drug testing policy mandates testing for all students in grades six through 12 who want to participate in extracurricular activities. Students who test positive are barred from extracurricular activities and must enroll in a drug assistance program.

In 1997, the first year the policy was implemented, 181 out of 500 high school students were tested and 90 out of 333 junior high students were tested, according to documents.

The policy was initiated after the school board hired The Search Institute of Minneapolis, Minn., to conduct a behavioral survey of all students in grades six through 12 in the district. According to the results, 63 percent of Trinidad seniors "reported using marijuana once in their lifetimes."

Carlos Lopez, a senior band member when the policy was started, refused to take the drug test, saying it violated the Fourth Amendment.

The U.S. Seventh Circuit Court of Appeals earlier last year upheld an Indiana school district's drug policy that required students to undergo random drug testing if they want to participate in extracurricular activities, or drive to school. The federal court said in *Todd v. Rush County Schools* (97-2548) that the policy is legal because it's meant to deter drug use. The Seventh Circuit based its opinion on *Vernonia*, as well.

High Court Turns Away Drug Test Case

The U.S. Supreme Court in August let stand lower federal court rulings on student drug testing.

On the first day of the Court's 1998-99 term, the justices without comment let stand a U.S. Seventh Circuit Court of Appeals ruling that a school's random drug testing for all students in extracurricular activities, even if they are not suspected of using drugs, does not violate students' privacy rights.

The Rush County, Ind., school board initiated a drug testing policy under which students in all extracurricular activities—whether the chess club or the football team—must submit to random drug testing. Two families appealed to the Supreme Court in *Todd v. Rush County Schools* (97-2021), saying the policy goes too far.

The Seventh Circuit, however, relied on a 1995 Supreme Court decision in *Vernonia v. Acton* (115 S.Ct. 2386) which said that deterring drug use among high school athletes served a "compelling interest to protect the health of students."

The High Court's action is not a ruling, and therefore doesn't set a national precedent, but it may bolster school districts' efforts to create similar policies.

Court Upholds Firing of Teacher Suspected of Drug Use

A federal appeals court in October ruled against a Georgia teacher who refused to take a drug test after marijuana was allegedly found in her car.

The Chatham County school board fired Sherry Hearn, a 27-year high school teacher, for refusing to take a drug test after a drug-sniffing dog allegedly found marijuana in her car while it was parked in a school lot.

She sued the school for violating her Fourth Amendment rights to due process by failing to gain her consent to search her car or obtain a search warrant. Hearn also said the school district had no right to fire her because she refused to take a drug test, opting to invoke her Fifth Amendment right not to incriminate herself.

'Probable Cause To Search'

But the appeals court agreed with a lower court that ruled against her.

"The alerting of a drug-sniffing dog to a person's property supplies not only reasonable suspicion, but probable cause to search that property," wrote Judge James Hill of the 11th Circuit Court of Appeals.

"When the property alerted to is in a vehicle, the Constitution permits a search of the vehicle immediately, without resort to a warrant," Hill said.

Hill also disagreed with Hearn's argument that her firing violated her Fifth Amendment rights.

"She contends that because the officer [read her her Miranda rights], she cannot be terminated for exercising her right to remain silent," he said, but "this argument is without merit."

"The production of body fluids is nontestimonial," Hill added. "Hearn has not offered any authority that the production of urine does not fall within this rule, nor do we know of any."

Hill concluded that Hearn was not forced to testify against herself in violation of the Fifth Amendment. Ultimately, Hill said her contract with the school board does not "vitiate the authority of the law enforcement officers to search her car under the circumstances of this case."

Teacher of the Year

In April 1996, school and county police officers conducted a random drug search at a Georgia high school. During the search, a drug-sniffing dog alerted police to Hearn's car, which was parked in a rear parking lot, unlocked with the passenger-side window down.

The officer let the dog enter the car through the passenger-side window, and the dog found what police would later discover was a marijuana cigarette.

After the officers informed both the principal and Hearn of their finding, she denied any knowledge of the drug. The officers read her her rights and told her she likely would be charged with criminal possession of drugs, but they did not press charges.

School officials told her that she must take a drug test within 48 hours, per school policy. Hearn, a teacher of constitutional law who was the 1994 Teacher of the Year, refused, ultimately resulting in her firing on insubordination grounds.

Judge Wilkie Ferguson, the lone dissenter in the 2-1 decision in *Hearn v. Board of Education* (98-8390), said a jury should decide whether the search of Hearn's car was lawful, particularly since they ultimately did not press charges.

Also, pointing to the absence of police charges, he noted that Hearn's contract protects her from searches of her desk, vehicle and other personal effects in matters that involve no criminal activity. "In my view, this fact-driven case should go to a jury," he said.

ACLU Sues Oklahoma District over Drug Testing

In a landmark suit touted as the first of its kind, two Oklahoma students are suing their school district over a policy that requires them to submit to drug tests in order to participate in extracurricular activities.

The American Civil Liberties Union (ACLU) is suing on behalf of students Lindsay Earls and Daniel James, who took school-mandated drug tests that were required for them to participate in extracurricular activities tied to regular education classes. The tests cost each student $5.

The testing is required for students who participate in activities that are tied to regular courses, such as debate, chorus and band. If students enroll in choir class during the regular school day, for example, they are required to participate in the corresponding extracurricular activity to receive credit for the class.

The Supreme Court in 1998 let stand a drug-testing policy in an Indiana school district that required random drug testing for all students participating in extracurricular activities.

But ACLU officials say the difference in the present suit is that some of the extracurricular activities are linked to academic courses. "A student can take the choir class only if she also participates in the extracurricular choir activities," says the suit, filed in August 1999. "Thus the drug-testing policy effectively applies to parts of a public school's core legally required function—the education of its students."

Courts have generally ruled that drug-testing is the price a student must pay to participate in extracurricular activities. "Testing anybody beyond athletes is a wide-open question," said ACLU attorney Graham Boyd. "What we're looking for here is a ruling, and it may come from the Supreme Court, saying you may not have random drug testing for students other than athletes."

Tecumseh school district attorney Linda Meoli denied that the drug-testing is linked in any way to participating in academic classes. She likened the policy to those in districts around the country.

The issue has been the subject of much debate, and the rulings across the country have been varied, with the circumstances under which drug-testing is required weighing heavily on whether courts agree to the policy.

For example, the Supreme Court in March let stand a federal court ruling that bans an Indiana school district from requiring all high school students who are suspended—regardless of the offense—to submit to drug tests before returning to school.

DRUG POLICY

State Court Upholds Utah Student's Drug Suspension

A state court upheld the suspension of a San Juan County, Utah, student who was accused of using drugs on a school trip.

Rory Atcitty, who claimed he was denied due process, sued the district after Whitehorse High School Principal Lyman Grover suspended him for refusing to tell whether he and other students used drugs while on a school trip.

In *Atcitty v. Board of Education of the San Juan County School District* (981096-CA), the Utah Court of Appeals ruled that the principal's failed attempts to query the boy and his parents on the matter was "all the due process owed to the appellant."

ALCOHOL POLICY

Court Upholds Suspension of Athlete Caught Drunk

A state appeals court ruled in March 1999 that school officials did not violate the civil rights of a student athlete suspended from sports for violating the school's ban on alcohol use.

"Students can, need, want and expect to participate in interscholastic athletics, but students are not entitled to participate in them," wrote Judge Clyde Kuehn of the Appellate Court of Illinois.

Student and star athlete Kevin Jordon said officials at O'Fallon Township High School violated his 14th Amendment rights to due process when they suspended him from sports for one season without a hearing for violating the school's zero-tolerance alcohol policy.

He said the school's action limited his ability to collect an athletic scholarship to college, and that he had a constitutional right to defend himself at a formal hearing. Although the 14th Amendment forbids the state from depriving any person of "life, liberty or property without due process of law," Kuehn said "to have a property interest in a benefit, a person must have more than an abstract need or desire for it."

"He must have a legitimate claim of entitlement to it," he said, referring to previous federal and state rulings on the matter. "Courts have repeatedly held that there is no property of liberty interest in taking part in interscholastic athletics."

Kevin's playing privileges were suspended for the 1998 football season after he called the police from a convenience store at 3 a.m. They found him drunk and reported that he admitted to drinking alcohol.

The officers reported the incident to school officials, who confronted Kevin. He denied the officer's version of events. But officials suspended him, concluding that Kevin—who was up for a number of athletic scholarships to be based on his performance in the 1998 season —had violated the school's ban on drug and alcohol use.

After an unsuccessful appeal to school system administrators, he unsuccessfully filed suit in an Illinois trial court to block his suspension from sports. Calling Kevin's argument "untenable," Kuehn agreed with the lower court also refusing to block his suspension.

"Since Jordan possessed no independent right to participate in high school football, the existence of a protected property interest depends upon whether he can legitimately claim the right to participate in order to earn college financial assistance," Kuehn wrote.

"This, in turn, depends upon whether the hope of earning a college scholarship rises to the level of a protectable property interest," he said. "Under the circumstances presented, it does not."

CHAPTER 10

Search and Seizure

Highly publicized incidents of school violence nationally have forced school officials to take more seriously students' threats of violence and rumors of students bearing weapons, or drugs.

Often, that means searching lockers, backpacks or students themselves. The result is a climate in which school officials—arguing that they have a responsibility to maintain a safe school environment—struggle against students asserting their right to privacy.

When the searches were limited to certain students, federal courts often sided with the schools, citing officials' responsibility to maintain safety and prevent tragedy on school grounds.

Legal experts point to a number of cases that guide school officials in how to conduct lawful searches of students.

The U.S. Supreme Court in the 1985 case *New Jersey v. T.L.O.* ruled that school officials need reasonable grounds to suspect that searching a student's personal effects will reveal evidence of a violation of law or school rules.

Jacqueline Stefkovich, a professor at Temple University, said while the high court's decision in *T.L.O.* did not address "mass and highly intrusive [strip] searches, courts and legal scholars have generally considered such searches illegal." But recently, more intrusive searches of students have been upheld, under some circumstances.

For example, in 1993 the 7th Circuit Court of Appeals ruled that high school officials who strip-searched a student for drugs after they noticed an over-sized bulge in his pants did not violate the boy's rights.

The court in *Cornfield v. Consolidated High School District No. 230* (92-1863) conceded that the event may have been traumatic for the boy, but the search did not violate the Fourth Amendment, which bars unreasonable searches.

More recently, in 1997, the high court refused to hear a case involving two second-grade girls who were strip-searched when school officials suspected them of stealing $7.

The U.S. 11th Circuit Court of Appeals in *Jenkins v. Herring* (115 F.3d 821) ruled that a strip search violated the Fourth Amendment, but school officials were immune from lawsuit because there was no legal precedence in 1992 to warn them that such searches were unconstitutional.

Meeting the "reasonable suspicion" standard set in *T.L.O.* may be a matter of hearing a rumor, or getting a tip from an anonymous informant, student or someone else, as a basis for questioning or ultimately searches, said Michigan school attorney Lisa Swem, of Thrun, Maatsch & Nordberg, at a law conference.

Two cases from the 6th Circuit Court of Appeals ruled that school officials may use hearsay testimony from an anonymous student in a discipline hearing because accused students do not have the right to face their accusers or know their identities.

The court, in *Parades v. Curtis, 864 F. 2d 426, 429* and *Newsome v. Batavia Local School District,* 842 F. 2d 920, 924-25), held it is more important to protect student informants—because they might witness crimes or violations—that it is to reveal their identities.

The overall issue, Swem said, is that sometimes schools can be sued and held liable when school staff are aware of a threat to students and fail to act.

"Some courts have even interpreted school efforts to curb violence as an assumption of heightened duty to supervise," Swem said. She stressed that schools aren't usually held liable for "sudden, unexpected violence" on campus, but they can be for incidents a jury sees as "foreseeable."

Legal experts suggest searches be limited and tied to reasonable suspicion, as was the case in the following:

- A federal court in Rhode Island in 1998 ruled in favor of school officials who searched a sixth grade girl by patting her down because they suspected she had a knife (*Brousseau v. Town of Westerly*; 11 F. Supp. 2d 177).

- A federal court in New York in 1999 upheld the search of students' rooms while they were on a class trip to Disney World because a school chaperone smelled marijuana. He found marijuana and alcohol in one student's room (*Rhodes v. Guarricino*; 98-2164).

- A federal court in 1997 ruled in favor of a Kansas school district when a student sued because officials, acting on a tip from a parent, searched the boy's car for a gun, and found one (*James v. Unified School District*; 959 F. Supp. 1407).

But cases often go against school districts when federal courts determine that a school district conducted an unreasonable search, Stevkovich said.

In one New Mexico case, a court determined that the school district conducted an "unreasonable search" when it strip-searched 10 students to find a missing ring.

The New Mexico Supreme Court ruled in *Kennedy v. Dexter Consolidated Schools* (955 P. 2d 693; 1998), that, although it was reasonable to conclude that one of the 10 girls likely lifted the ring, the group was too large for each of its members to be considered individually suspect.

DRUGS AND WEAPONS

Rumor Sparked Legal Search of Student, Court Says

A Pennsylvania court ruled that school officials acting on an anonymous police tip did not violate the rights of a student suspected of having a weapon when they asked him to empty his pockets.

Before the case went to trial, a middle school student, only identified in court records as D.E.M., tried to block police from using evidence collected by school officials after he complied with a request that he empty his pockets. Schools officials found that the boy had a sheathed knife, and then the boy admitted to having a loaded gun in a jacket he left in a friend's locker.

School officials, who were required by school policy to investigate the rumor and report any weapons finding to the police, searched the locker and found the gun.

But D.E.M. said the search violated his Fourth Amendment rights to be free from unreasonable search and seizure. He said school officials had no right to detain him because they had no basis to suspect he had weapons before police gave them the tip.

The Pennsylvania Superior Court overturned a 1997 ruling from a lower court that said school officials violated D.E.M's rights by becoming agents of the police when they, acting on the police tip, detained D.E.M. and searched the locker with no independent suspicion of the weapons possession.

"We hold that school officials do not act as agents of the police where they conduct an independent investigation based upon information the officials received from police," wrote Judge John Kelly March in the March 1999 opinion of the three-judge panel.

"We also hold that school officials do not need reasonable suspicion, supported by specific and articulable facts, before merely detaining and questioning a student about a rumor concerning his possession of a gun on school property," wrote Kelly, granting the state's request to allow the use of the weapons evidence.

"Finally, we hold that school officials need not provide Miranda warnings to a student before questioning the student about conduct that violates the law and/or school rules," Kelly concluded.

The decision was based on a number of rulings, including the 1985 Supreme Court opinion in *New Jersey v. T.L.O.* (469 U.S. 325, 105 S. Ct. 733, 83 L.Ed.2d 720).

T.L.O. said school officials must base their searches of students' personal effects on "reasonable suspicion" that the search would reveal evidence of a violation of law or school rule.

School officials may generally rely on tips from either a student informant or another reliable source, and school officials generally are not required to reveal the informant's identity.

No Clear Road Map

Legal experts say rulings on the issue vary so greatly across the country that school officials should look carefully at the rules applying to their respective jurisdictions.

"When it comes to case law on this, decisions are all over the map," said Lisa Swem, an attorney specializing in school law for Thrun, Maatsch & Nordberg.

"Some courts find that school officials need only meet the reasonable suspicion standard set in *T.L.O.* to conduct a search, but the more it looks like school officials are acting like agents of the police, the more courts apply the higher standard of probable cause," she said.

School officials are forced to determine whether and how to act on rumors because they may be held liable for failing to act on information that could create a safety concern or be a violation of laws or school rules, Swem said.

"They have to balance their duty to act versus whether they have a constitutional basis to search a student locker."

Limited Privacy Rights

But Kelly said students' right to privacy in school is limited, especially when school safety is at risk.

"In any realistic sense, students within the school environment have a lesser expectation of privacy than members of the population generally," Kelly wrote in *Commonwealth of Pennsylvania v. D.E.M* (1999 PA Super 59).

"It is simply unrealistic to think that students have the same subjective expectation of privacy as the population generally," he wrote, also mentioning school officials' duty to ensure the safety of students.

And in light of the national spate of school shootings in recent years, particularly last month's massacre at a Colorado high school, legal experts say school officials aren't likely to ignore a rumor about a student carrying a weapon in school.

"The Superior Court got it right when it said it doesn't matter where a tip comes from," said Edwin Darden, a staff attorney at the National School Boards Association.

"It's a matter of schools acting responsibly to protect student safety, and in this case the police gave the schools a tip and then walked away," Darden said.

"There was no coercion or police involvement until school officials reported their findings to police."

Drug-Sniffing Canine Did Not Trump Student's Privacy

The search and detainment of a high school student was not illegal after a drug-sniffing dog stopped him at school, a federal appeals court has ruled.

The U.S. 9th Circuit Court of Appeals in October 1999 affirmed a lower court ruling that Plumas Unified School District in California has 11th Amendment immunity from being sued for damages in this case. The amendment protects the government from being sued except in cases of gross negligence.

Judge Harry Pregerson said the 1996 search was legal, even though school officials violated students' "reasonable expectation of privacy." But in this case, even a search that trumps privacy is reasonable when there is a government interest in conducting it, such as keeping schools drug-free, he ruled for the three-judge panel.

Quincy High School officials were notified that police officials would comb the school with a drug-sniffing dog on May 21, 1996, and directed students not to leave their classrooms. When a student only identified in court records as B.C. and other students left despite that instruction, they were directed to a covered snack-bar area.

Routine Search

Deputy Sheriff Dean Canalia escorted Keesha, a drug-sniffing dog, through the halls of the school during the routine drug search. B.C. was among a group of students Keesha sniffed out, indicating the likelihood of narcotics.

The students were told to stay out of the classroom while the dog sniffed their belongings. When they were told to return, Keesha sniffed out a student other than B.C., and that student was taken to another room and searched. Police found no drugs at the school that day.

B.C., on behalf of himself and five other students, sued the school, saying the "sniff and search" violated their Fourth Amendment right to be free of unreasonable search and seizure.

But Judge Pregerson denied B.C.'s request for damages and to have the case, *Powers v. Plumas Unified School District* (9717287v2), classified as a class-action, which would have allowed the suit to represent multiple plaintiffs affected by the allegation.

He said school and police officials could only be held liable if it was proved that the police officials used the dog to search students despite knowing it would constitute an unlawful search. In the current case, the dog sniffed the students while passing them in a hall, and Pregerson said B.C. did not demonstrate that he would be subject to an "illegal dog sniff again," or that the sniff constituted a search.

Dissenting Judge Melvin Brunetti pointed to Supreme Court and 9th Circuit precedents that do not support the majority's argument that students have a reasonable expectation of privacy in school.

Kentucky Student Sues over Drug Search, Suspension

A Kentucky high school senior is suing his school district for suspending him and banning him from the prom after officials allegedly found marijuana in his truck.

But courts in the past several years have ruled against students fighting similar drug enforcement policies.

"The courts in recent years have given school districts much more lee-way and control in searching students and their property for drugs," said Julie Underwood, general counsel for the National School Boards Association. "Cases like these are more prevalent, but the students are losing."

Irvine, Ky., police found a small amount of marijuana in Darren Baker's truck during a random drug search that included a drug-sniff-ing dog. But Baker, 17, says he never got a hearing on the drug charge before being suspended from school for three days and being banned from the prom and a senior trip to Washington, DC.

The school's drug policy requires an automatic suspension for stu-dents caught with drugs, said Estill County Superintendent Tom Bonny.

Though he refrains from discussing Darren's case for privacy reasons, he said his school division holds hearings for all students involved in serious infractions, as required by state law.

Because his district helped purchase a $4,000 drug-sniffing dog, Bonny said school officials three years ago agreed to let local police conduct ran-dom drug searches in the 2,800-student, five-school district.

Paul Armentano, spokesman for the Washington, D.C.-based Na-tional Organization for the Reform of Marijuana Laws, said school districts "more and more are breaching students' Fourth Amendment rights even when they have no evidence of epidemic drug use at school.

"It was not too long ago that random searches and drug dogs in schools would have been abhorrent and considered unconstitu-tional," he said.

The Fourth Amendment protects citizens from unreasonable search and seizure. But Underwood said courts have held that schools "have to make their premises safe for students, so students are not deemed as having the same right to privacy as a citizen would with a police officer."

The U.S. Supreme Court in October turned away several appeals of school drug testing policies, letting stand lower federal court rulings allowing random drug testing in schools.

In Darren's case, school officials have not responded to the suit filed Nov. 13.

Signs of Drug Use Justified School Exam, Court Rules

A high school student's bloodshot eyes, dilated pupils and giddy behavior were ample reason for an administrator to have the school nurse evaluate him for marijuana use, a federal appeals court ruled.

Even though a subsequent drug test showed the student was clean, the administrator's actions were reasonable because she is a certified drug counselor and the boy's symptoms could have indicated drug use, the court said in a November 1997 ruling.

The U.S. Seventh Circuit Court of Appeals ruled that giving the boy an impromptu "medical assessment" in school didn't violate the Fourth Amendment, which protects individuals from unreasonable searches.

"The medical assessment was reasonably calculated to uncover further evidence of the suspected drug use," the court ruled in *Bridgman v. New Trier High School District No. 203* (97-1412).

What's Wrong with Your Eyes?

Andrew Bridgman was a freshman when the school required him to attend an after-school smoking cessation program because he'd been caught smoking cigarettes around school at least twice. Mary Dailey supervised the program.

In the session, Dailey said Bridgman behaved inappropriately, giggling and acting unruly. She said his eyes were bloodshot and pupils dilated, and his handwriting was "erratic."

Dailey took the student into another room and accused him of being under the influence of drugs, which he denied. She then took him to the school nurse, who checked his blood pressure and pulse and found them "considerably higher" than those listed on his freshman medical exam.

The school nurse said she didn't think Bridgman was acting strangely and didn't notice anything wrong with his eyes. Dailey told Bridgman to take off his hat, outer jersey, shoes and socks, and to empty his pockets. He did so, and no drugs were found.

Bridgman's mother offered to take him to a pediatrician the next day and had him tested for drugs. The school agreed that the test showed the boy had not used marijuana.

The family sued the school district and Dailey, contending the medical assessment violated the Fourth Amendment. The school and family presented conflicting expert testimony about whether bloodshot eyes, rapid pulse and dilated pupils indicate marijuana use.

But the three-judge appeals court panel agreed unanimously with a district court that Dailey's actions were reasonable, based on her observations.

The appeals court cited its 1993 ruling in *Cornfield v. Consolidated High School District No. 230* (991 F.2d 1316), in which it permitted male school employees to strip-search a male student for drugs.

In the latest case, the court said, Dailey did not touch the boy, and he was not forced to remove all his clothing.

"The search was not excessively intrusive in relation to its purpose," the judges said in dismissing the suit.

MIRANDA RIGHTS

School Officials Do Not Have To *'Miranda'* Students

School officials are not required to inform students of their legal rights when questioning them about alleged misconduct on school property, a Rhode Island court has ruled.

"The weight of authority is that *Miranda* warnings are necessary only when a defendant is subject to questioning by law enforcement officials, their agents, and agents of the court while the suspect is in official custody," the Rhode Island Supreme Court said.

The state high court ruled that a student, identified in court records as Harold S., was not entitled to hear his legal rights when the principal called him to his office to question him about his involvement in a fight at school.

The court also ruled that Harold S.'s statements to Thomas Middle School Principal Rodrigo Borgueta are admissible in court. Harold S. admitted hitting another student at the Newport, R.I., school.

Harold S. at first denied assaulting a student during a fight when he and his father met with Borgueta in the principal's office. But then he conceded orally and in writing that he hit the victim because the victim "touched [Harold S.'s] butt."

Following school policy, the principal later submitted the statement to the police, who then pressed assault charges against the youth.

But Harold S. argued in Family Court that he should have been informed of his Miranda rights before the principal—who, Harold S. claimed, was then acting as an agent of the police—questioned him, and before he made the written statement that was turned over to the police.

The *Miranda* warning took effect in 1966, when the Supreme Court ruled that law enforcement officials must immediately inform a person placed under arrest of his or her constitutional rights, such as the right to remain silent.

The student said the meeting with the principal "amounted to a police interrogation in a coercive environment," according to court records.

The trial judge denied that motion, saying no constitutional violation had occurred. The student then appealed to the Rhode Island Supreme Court, which affirmed the lower court's ruling last June.

"Because the principal was not acting as an agent of the police when he questioned respondent and because respondent was not subjected to a custodial interrogation by law-enforcement authorities, it was unnecessary to inform [him] of his rights prior to this questioning," the state high court ruled in *Harold S. v Thompson Middle School* (98-139).

CHAPTER 11

Other

CORPORAL PUNISHMENT

Alabama Court Holds Teacher Liable in Student Paddling

An Alabama appeals court says a teacher went too far—too far even in a state that sanctions corporal punishment—when she paddled a student for using the word "ass."

The Court of Civil Appeals of Alabama ordered teacher Jacqueline Hinson of Tallassee City Schools to pay the boy $5,000, plus court costs.

Tallassee school policy allows teachers to administer corporal punishment without advising the principal in three situations: for essential self-defense, to preserve order and to protect others. But school policy states that the measure should be used only as a last resort.

The September 1995 beating occurred after Hinson, a physical education instructor, overheard 13-year-old Dustin Holt saying, "I will kick your ass." Dustin claimed that one of his classmates asked him to repeat a comment made by another student.

The family sued Hinson and the Tallassee City Schools after Holt came home from school with large bruises on his buttocks and was unable to sit for several days.

In upholding a lower court decision in *Hinson v. Holt* (2970541), Judge

William Robertson said Hinson acted "with legal malice in punishing Dustin" for what is "at most, a mildly profane reference."

In delivering the November 1999 decision of the five-member court, the judge said the teacher violated not only school policy, but Dustin's right to due process when she struck him three times.

School Escapes Unscathed

Although the Holts sued the city schools and Hinson in her official and individual capacities, the Elmore Circuit Court ruled that the district was protected under government immunity.

Hinson argued that she also should be immune from legal action. She is asking the full five-member Alabama appeals court to review the ruling.

CURRICULUM CONTENT

Go Ask the Superintendent: Court Lets School Ban Song

A federal district court has ruled that a Missouri school superintendent can legally bar a school band from playing a song he believes endorses illegal drug use.

The decision of the U.S. District Court for the Eastern District of Missouri became final in August 1999 after students from the Fort Zumalt North High School Marching Band opted not to appeal the decision.

The court ruled that since the marching band is part of the fall curriculum for the high school course "Symphonic Band," Superintendent Bernard DeBray has the legal authority to ban the song from any school-sponsored activity.

Band director Robert Babel selected "White Rabbit" by Jefferson Airplane as part of the marching band's musical arrangements for the 1998-99 school year's performances and competitions.

Although they would not have been heard during a performance, the song's lyrics contain references from *Alice In Wonderland*, such as a hookah-smoking caterpillar and the words, "One pill makes you larger, and one pill makes you small." Babel said the song was consistent with this year's theme: popular rock music from the late 1960s and early 1970s.

Students enrolled in Symphonic Band are required to be members of the marching band and earn a grade based on their performance. Because of that, the court agreed with the school district's decision.

Feed Your Head?

Judge Rodney Sippel based his decision on the U.S. Supreme Court's 1988 opinion in *Hazelwood School District v. Kuhlmeir* (484 U.S. 260, 266).

In that case, the high court held that school officials may restrict "the style and content of student speech in school-sponsored expressive activities so long as their actions are reasonably related to legitimate pedagogical concerns."

The high court said school officials must have the authority to determine what is harmful to students as they teach them "cultural values" and prepare them "for later professional training."

But the *Hazelwood* court specified which activities fall into that legal category: "school-sponsored publications, theatrical productions, and other expressive activities that students, parents and members of the public might reasonably perceive to bear the imprimatur of the school … whether or not they occur in a traditional classroom setting, so long as they are supervised by faculty members and designed to impart particular knowledge or skills to student participants or audiences."

The students' attorney, Joseph Green, asked the district court to clarify whether, under *Hazelwood*, the school could ban "White Rabbit" or other songs deemed inappropriate from extracurricular activities that do not earn letter grades, such as talent contests.

"The court told us that those cases would have to be taken up on a case-by-case basis, since activities that do not earn letter grades may not be covered under *Hazelwood*," Green said, adding that he told the students not to appeal the current decision because it rests on solid legal ground.

But, Green added, "I told the students that if school officials ban a song like that—in an activity that is not part of the main curriculum—I will be happy to test the bounds of *Hazelwood* in a censorship case." For now, the opinion in *McCann v. Fort Zumalt School District* (98-1790) is final.

Connecticut: School Liability Likely in Pupil-Distress Case

A Connecticut appeals court has ruled that a school district may be liable for inflicting emotional distress on students exposed to a curriculum that apparently induced chaos and violence in classrooms.

The Appellate Court of Connecticut said on Oct. 26, 1999, that the curriculum, which emphasized social skills over academics, may have caused emotional harm to children. The court overturned a lower court ruling that had dismissed this claim.

In September 1994, Ellen Fenty-Morrison, the principal at Alma Pagels School in West Haven, introduced a curriculum created by the Northeast Foundation for Children.

Morrison, who also worked for the foundation, maintained the program at the school through June 1996 with funds earmarked for curriculum development by West Haven's school board.

The board gave its schools no direction on how to use the money, court records show.

The program rewarded children for proper social behavior instead of academic improvements. Ultimately, it resulted in students losing focus on their school work and causing class disruption instead.

Fenty-Morrison, who publicly stated that she adopted the program because she does not believe in "rewarding academic excellence," was the only principal in the district to use the method throughout her school, though teachers at other schools reportedly used the program in a limited capacity.

Alma Pagels School parents sued the school district because the program not only failed to improve social skills, but also denied students the benefits of a traditional education by exposing them to chaos, disruption and violence when teachers failed to regain control of their classes.

Despite these problems, the school kept the program for two school years, court records show.

The parents said their children ultimately were deprived of the kind of education given to students at other elementary schools in West Haven and in the state. The parents sued for money damages on three counts of educational malpractice, three counts of negligence and three counts of intentional infliction of emotional distress.

But state Appellate Court Judge Sidney Landau, writing for the three-judge panel, affirmed the New Haven Superior Court's ruling dismissing the six counts of educational malpractice and negligence.

Each court based its decision on state and federal rulings that require plaintiffs seeking money damages in such cases to prove an institution failed in some basic aspect to offer courses needed to achieve certification in a subject area.

The second legal standard is proving that the school failed to fulfill a contractual obligation aside from any general obligation within a program. "Under the facts of this case, the plaintiffs' claims of educational malpractice [and negligence] do not survive the defendants' motion to strike," Landau wrote.

Emotional Distress Revisited

But Landau reversed the lower court's dismissal of the emotional distress claims in *Bell v. Board of Education of the City of West Haven* (18207).

The parents claimed that, as a result of being exposed to the curriculum, their kids are afraid of schoolteachers, tests and other students.

Landau said this element of the parents' claim should not have been dismissed because it meets the three legal standards necessary to establish liability. The principal, and hence the district, should have known that emotional distress was the likely outcome of exposing the children to a "chaotic" program for two years, he wrote.

He said that the school district's and the principal's failure to remove the program expeditiously amounted to extreme and outrageous behavior, and that the children likely have sustained severe emotional distress.

"We can think of no reason why our society could or should countenance or suffer this type of conduct in a place of learning," Landau wrote, in ordering the lower court to review the case again.

CONTAGIOUS DISEASES

Student Wrestler Can Sue over Herpes Transmission

The Supreme Court of New York is allowing a student wrestler to proceed with a lawsuit alleging that a teammate knowingly infected him with a transmittable disease during a practice match.

Joseph Silver filed the complaint after a Nov. 30, 1996, incident, during which Silver, a member of the Division Avenue High School wrestling team, was called to practice with Daniel Patascher. Patascher was a former member of the wrestling team who graduated from high school in 1996. He was observing the practice.

Silver's complaint alleges that his coach directed him to wrestle with Patascher, and as a result, he came into contact with Patascher's herpes simplex virus, a highly contagious disease that causes sores and blisters around the head and face.

The complaint also asserts that Patascher was negligent for "recklessly and/or intentionally failing to inform the plaintiff ... that he suffered from [the virus]."

Patascher argued that there is no valid complaint for the "negligent transmission of a disease through casual contact." But state Judge Sandra Feuerstein said she does not view the incident in this case as "casual contact."

"[T]he complaint sufficiently states a cause of action for negligent transmission of herpes simplex," Feuerstein wrote in February 1999.

"The plaintiff has alleged that the defendant knew of this condition and wrestled with the plaintiff without disclosing the condition."

State law recognizes lawsuits stemming from both negligent and intentional transmission of communicable diseases.

Patascher had a responsibility to disclose his disease, because wresting requires "participants to be in very intimate contact with each other," Feuerstein wrote in *Silver v. Levittown Union Free School District* (98-314).

BOOK BANNING

Appeals Court Won't Ban Books Because of Racial Harassment

A federal appeals has refused to order an Arizona school district to remove from the curriculum books that a parent blames for racial hostility by white students.

While the U.S. Ninth Circuit Court of Appeals found no link between the books the black parent found offensive and the harassment, it did order a lower court to review whether the school district violated federal antidiscrimination laws by failing to stop the harassment.

Kathy Monteiro wanted the court to force Tempe Union High School District to remove immediately Mark Twain's "Adventures of Huckleberry Finn" and William Faulkner's "A Rose for Emily" from the mandatory curriculum. She says the assignments for her freshman daughter's English class caused white students to repeatedly call the girl and other black students "nigger."

"Monteiro alleges that racial harassment, including verbal insults, increased, 'as a result of' the assignment of [the books], but [that] link is wholly unsupported by any factual allegations," Judge Stephen Reinhardt wrote for the unanimous three-judge panel in *Monteiro v. Tempe Union High School District* (97-15511), decided in October 1998.

But Reinhardt said if racial harassment increased, "there are many other more likely causes that all of the interested parties might do well to explore. Bad ideas should be countered with good ones, not banned by the courts."

Monteiro said school officials dismissed her daughter's complaints of white students' racist conduct, violating the girl's rights under Title VI of the 1964 Civil Rights Act and her constitutional right to equal protection. Title VI bans racial discrimination in federally funded institutions.

The United States District Court for the District of Arizona dismissed Monteiro's civil rights complaints, but the appeals court ordered the lower court to review that claim in November 1999, pointing to U.S. Supreme Court rulings that hold school districts liable for damages when officials are aware of discrimination but fail to act.

"The district is liable for its failure to act if the need for intervention was so obvious," Reinhardt wrote, citing Monteiro's allegations of "a pattern of egregious public racial harassment including the use of the epithet 'nigger,' that black students and their parents complained but were rebuffed, and that nothing was ever done about the problem."

Judge Robert Boochever, in a separate opinion, said had the books contained "overt messages of racial hatred, such as those promoting the views of the Aryan Nation, the Ku Klux Klan, or similar hate groups," removing them from the curriculum may have been appropriate. The U.S. District Court for the District of Arizona has not yet reviewed the ruling.?

HOME SCHOOLING

Head Massachusetts Court Blocks At-Home School Monitoring

Massachusetts' school districts have no right to enter the homes of parents who home-school their children to monitor how they teach, the state's highest court ruled.

A school district's policy on home schooling must be "essential and reasonable," the state supreme court ruled in its unanimous decision to uphold parents' "basic right to educate their children."

Public schools may conduct home visits when a child is failing academically, or if families send their children to school at a neighbor's home, the court ruled, but other home visits are not essential.

The December 1998 ruling in *Brunelle, et al. v. Lynn Public Schools* (SJC-07709) ended a seven-year battle in the state over parents' rights to teach their children versus the responsibility of public school officials to ensure they receive an adequate education.

Although the ruling applies strictly to schools in Massachusetts, a home school advocate says it may help settle a long-running debate across the country.

Districts' 'Harassment Arsenal'

"The ruling makes home visits a non-issue, taking it off the table as part of school district's harassment arsenal," said Michael Farris, the attorney who represented the parents and heads the Purcellville, Va.-based Home School Legal Defense Fund.

"It is a dying practice, but we've seen the pendulum swing in that direction in a number of states," he said. New York, Pennsylvania, Rhode Island and South Dakota had similar policies, he said, and some have tried to impose teacher testing of parents who home school. "But we have beat back a number of those in court."

Naomi Gittins, staff attorney for the National School Boards Association, said it is fairly uncommon for a school district to ask to visit home-schoolers.

In 1994, Michael and Virginia Brunelle, who home school their five children, faced criminal charges under truancy laws when they refused to submit their educational plans to Lynn public school officials and allow home visits.

When the charges were dropped, the Brunelles and another family that had initially filed suit against the schools in 1991 continued to challenge Lynn's policy. Federal courts ruled that it was a state issue.

Farris said state and local requirements on home schooling vary, from asking parents to seek curriculum approval by local school boards to notifying a board of the intention to home school. Most school systems require some type of documentation, such as lesson plans or test scores, proving that a student is being taught for the full school year.

The Massachusetts justices did not rule on the constitutionality of

Lynn's policy, but did say that no state law authorizes districts to require home visits.

Lynn officials were revamping their policy before the ruling and will not appeal the decision.

Table of Cases